EMOTIONAL INTELLIGENCE AND SELF-COMPASSION

2-in-1 Book

Discover How to Positively Embrace Your Negative Emotions and Improve Your Social Skill, Even if You're Constantly Too Hard on Yourself

EMOTIONAL INTELLIGENCE

Understand Your Emotions and Create Profound Relationships

Discover How To Develop Emotional Awareness, EQ, and Social Intelligence, Even If You're a Clueless Begineer

Table of Contents

Introduction 7

Chapter 1: What is Emotional Intelligence? 9

    Emotionally Intelligent Character Traits 13

Chapter 2: Emotional Intelligence in Daily Life 18

Chapter 3: Building Self-Awareness Skills 28

Chapter 4: Building Self-Management Skills 45

Chapter 5: Building Social Awareness Skills 57

Chapter 6: Building Relationship Management Skills 66

    Identifying and Analyzing a Relationship 67

    How to Practice Relationship Management 70

    How to Manage Different Types of Relationships 81

    Other Tips for Managing Relationships 84

Conclusion 90

Congratulations on purchasing *Emotional intelligence 2.0: A Practical Guide for Beginners* and thank you for doing so. Every effort was made to ensure it is full of as much useful information as possible. Please enjoy!

Introduction

You have heard so much about emotional intelligence that your interest is piqued. Whether you are a top-management official at work or a stay-at-home mom, emotional intelligence is important in your life. I commend you for taking the steps to develop your emotional intelligence skills. By doing so, you will only improve your quality of life from how you feel about yourself to how you feel about others, and ultimately, how others feel about you.

The following chapters will discuss how you can develop your ability to master emotional intelligence and to see great improvements in your personal and professional life. The book is divided into 6 easy-to-read chapters that will give you insight into how to manage your emotional intelligence.

The first chapter will give a brief overview of what emotional intelligence is. Then the subsequent chapters will break down the tenets of emotional intelligence into more detail. Chapter 2 builds on Chapter 1 and explores what emotional intelligence looks like in your everyday life. From this chapter, we dive right into building skills that will help you improve your emotional intelligence. In Chapter 3, how to manage your emotions will be discussed, followed by how to improve your self-awareness in Chapter 4. Chapter 5 explains how to use social awareness and relationship management respectively.

At the end of every chapter, there will be a special section dedicated to giving you skills on how to develop each skill in order to become better at emotional intelligence. Also, please note that throughout the chapters, you will learn about Valerie who does not have an idea about emotional intelligence and her socially bankrupt life reflects it. Please do not be like Valerie!

Hopefully, by the end of this book, you will learn a lot from Valerie on what to do and what not to do in regards to emotional intelligence. At the end of the chapter, bullet points of the chapter topics and activities you can do to help develop your emotional intelligence will be given. Take small baby steps and do not be afraid to feel awkward as you try to implement the changes associated with emotional intelligence into your life. Every journey must start with one step and it is difficult before it gets easier. By the time you finish, you will notice how much your life has improved just because you decided to take the step to be more emotionally intelligent.

There are plenty of books on this subject on the market, so thanks again for choosing this one! Every effort was made to ensure it is full of as much useful information as possible. Please enjoy!

Chapter 1: What is Emotional Intelligence?

Meet Valerie. Valerie is a typical American who is married with two kids, a house, and a white picket fence. Oh yeah, she has a beautiful black Labrador as well. Valerie would consider her to have an average level of emotional intelligence. She does ok at work. Her familial, personal, and professional relationships are so-so. She feels like she's walking through life. Not going fast or slow, but just regular shmegular. She doesn't always feel in control and sometimes has panic attacks because she is overwhelmed, stressed, and unhealthy. She figures everyone else is going through the same things so it is not a big problem.

Cut to one busy day where Valerie is rushing to work because she has not communicated to her family members that she needs help and all of the chores and housework falls on her. Not too mention, she had to stay late at work the night before because she is a people pleaser which made her oversleep in the first place. Picture Valerie in a car, speeding down the highway in the rain before she hydroplanes smack dab into an eighteen-wheeler. Her car spins out of control and Valerie finds herself pinned behind her steering wheel in her car that is sideways in a ditch. Of course, a Good Samaritan saw the incident and immediately called emergency services who rushed to the scene. After the paramedics help her out the car, she is whisked to the hospital.

The good news is, she was alive. The bad news is, she has amnesia and she has to learn everything all over again. Facts like her children's names, her husband's name, and her dog's name will be seemingly easy to learn. However, the nuances of emotional intelligence seemed much more difficult to learn. She has to learn how to identify her personal emotions, manage them when reacting to other people, as well as managing her social settings and relationships. Whew! Valerie is on a quest to relearn what emotional intelligence is, but Valerie is not alone. There are a lot of people who want to learn how to be emotionally intelligent and are on the same path as Valerie.

This book attempts to help people like Valerie and the readers navigate the tricky, topsy-turvy, abstract world of emotions and the unspoken rules that come with it. Unlike Valerie who is starting with a blank slate, most people have some type of experience with their emotions whether they have anger issues, are people pleasers, or are narcissists. Emotional intelligence draws upon your personal preferences and experiences to figure out how to survive in the world. In order to improve upon one's emotional intelligence, one must first understand what emotional intelligence is.

So what is emotional intelligence? Known in short as EI, emotional intelligence is the multi-faceted capacity of being in tune with your personal thoughts and emotions and being able to manage them in your daily living and in your dealings with other people. In order to be emotionally intelligent, you must first have mastery of who you are and know how to handle your emotions. Then you must know how to navigate relationships with other people, especially how to interpret and understand their emotions and how to be savvy in the way you respond to their emotions for optimal results. In other words, to be emotionally intelligent, you need to know what to say, when to say it, and how to say it. Sounds like a lot? You're right. Becoming emotionally intelligent can be overwhelming, but it is not impossible. It is a skill that can be learned with practice. Being emotionally intelligent is a trait many want to acquire because research has shown that emotionally intelligent people are deemed better leaders, better friends, and better family members. People with emotional intelligence do not necessarily have the highest IQ, but they understand how people work. As a result, their acumen in dealing with people helps them to be successful in a way that people who are not emotionally intelligent are not able to achieve.

Emotional intelligence was brought to the mainstream in 1995 by Daniel Goleman when he wrote the book *Emotional Intelligence: Why It Can Matter More Than IQ*. This book was seminal in changing how people thought about the power of emotions. Before this book, emotions were not seen as powerful tools to help you succeed. Emotions were seen as a hindrance. Goldman brought the importance of being emotionally intelligent to the forefront, but it was not an idea that originated with him. Way back in the day, over 2,000 years ago, Plato wrote that "All learning has an emotional base." Even though Plato had said that emotions were important centuries earlier, scientists did not always see it that way. However, in the 1920s, the idea that emotions were important re-emerged when Edward Thorndike named the ability to get along with others as "social intelligence."

In 1950, Abraham Maslow sparked the human potential movement and wrote about the importance of people enhancing their mental, physical, emotional, and spiritual strengths. From his research, lots of similar movements were launched and people began to build on his ideas. From this birth of new knowledge, two researchers, Peter Salovey and John "Jack" Mayer in the 1990s, have been credited with first using the term 'emotional intelligence.' In the article, Salovey and Mayer defined emotional intelligence as scientifically testable "intelligence." This work set the foundation for Daniel Goleman's book in 1995. From there, many different offshoots of emotional intelligence were developed. For the purpose of this book, we will focus on emotional intelligence as being composed of four different parts consisting of self-management, self-awareness, social awareness, and relationship management.

Self-awareness is being in tune with your emotions. If you are self-aware, you are great at identifying and deciphering your emotions and using them effectively when you react to a situation. Self-management is the act of managing your emotions and the reactions to any situation you may find yourself in. The word 'manage' is key in the definition of self-management. If you are great at self-management, it does not mean that you do not get angry or experience emotions at all. It means that you are adept at how you manage those emotions to get the outcome you want. Social awareness is being keen to the social environment around you. And relationship management is all about handling your relationships whether they be professional, personal, or even the relationship with yourself. In later chapters, each separate component will be delved into in greater detail.

To understand how one learns about emotional intelligence, a person must understand how our brains work. Our brain is divided into three separate parts — the basal ganglia, limbic system, and neocortex. The basal ganglia are at the root of our brain and it is considered the place where all our instincts reside. When you feel something in your gut, the information travels directly to this region of your brain without going through the other regions. This is information that you do not have to think about at all. The next part of the brain is the limbic system. The information processed by this part of your brain is considered to be processed on the subconscious level. Subconscious level information is a step above unconscious information and that information is right below our level of awareness. The subconscious level is where our emotions reside. It stores information about experiences good and bad that affect our behaviors, as well as it stores our value judgments. The neocortex is the next part of the brain. It controls your level of awareness. The information in this part of the brain is able to be accessed at will. It controls our reasoning, language, and thoughts. This brief overview of the brain is helpful to understand because certain activities suggested later on in the book target certain aspects of the brain. It is a cool tidbit to understand how the activities strengthen certain aspects of your brain so you can learn how to control your emotional intelligence better and be more aware.

Emotional Intelligence

Emotionally Intelligent Character Traits

How does someone who is emotionally intelligent act? People who are emotionally intelligent normally have a few characteristics that let others know they are emotionally intelligent individuals.

- Emotionally intelligent people have empathy. They are able to understand how others are feeling in any given situation. In other words, like the cliché says, emotionally intelligent people are able to walk in someone else's shoes. They are able to understand how someone with a sick child may be having a rough time or understand the importance of being nice to everyone whether they have experienced that situation or not.

- Emotional intelligent people also think deeply about their emotions and other people's emotions – a lot. They are pros at knowing how to relate and manipulate to other people in order to get the best outcome possible.

- Emotionally intelligent people do not run from criticism. They are able to take feedback easily without being defensive. They are able to take what people say about them, dissect the criticism, and take from the criticism what they may.

- Emotionally intelligent people are also genuine people. They seek authenticity in their relationships with other people and tend to see the best in people. Hence, they also are able to forgive and forget slights against them rather easily.

- People who are emotionally intelligent are very positive. They are not angels. However, they are effective at refocusing their thoughts, so they do not act impulsively and do something that they will regret later.

- Emotionally intelligent people do not run from confrontation. They face the criticism head-on and then go from there. They handle the conflict with ease, even if their egos are wounded in the process.

- Emotionally intelligent people are excellent communicators. They know their personality type and communication style and are able to effectively communicate with others and know the style in which they prefer to be communicated.

People who are not emotionally intelligent tend to be the exact opposite.

- They are easily flustered and easily angered.

- They are selfish and they only care about one person - themselves.

- They do not think before they speak and they talk all the time without any care to how other people may react to what they are saying.

- People who are not emotionally intelligent are usually not the easiest people to get along with.

Emotionally intelligent people are leagues ahead of people who are not emotionally intelligent. Interestingly, one can have characteristics of being emotionally intelligent and also have characteristics of not being emotionally intelligent. The key is to try and work on your emotional intelligence until you are competent in all four areas of being emotionally intelligent. This takes work.

Emotional Intelligence

For someone who has never ever thought about learning more about emotional intelligence, the information explained thus far may seem suspect. You may be one of the people who believe that emotional intelligence is a fluke. You may think that it is not necessary or important to be in tune with your emotions or in tune with the emotions of others in order to be a better person. You may think emotional intelligence is nothing but hippy-dippy foolery that has no place in the same sentence with rational thought. You may think that emotional intelligence has no effect on your success. However, think of that one person that you would not rather be around. This person always makes inappropriate jokes. They never know what to say. It is like they always have a foot in their mouth. These types of people have no self-awareness. No one wants to be around them. This is why emotional intelligence matters. There is no black-and-white version of emotional intelligence.

It is possible that you are good with some of the aspects of emotional intelligence and you need help controlling the other aspects. Perhaps you are good at knowing your feelings and you're able to manage your emotions, but you are terrible at communicating with others. Hence, your relationship management needs work. Perhaps you are excellent at navigating relations and social settings, whether they are professional or personal because you are great at putting on a front but your personal life is in shambles. You may need to work on your self-awareness. Or perhaps, you can easily be wonderful at managing other people's relationships. You can be the one friend that everyone comes to when they need help, but you are horrible at your own self-management. It happens. Just because you are okay with three out of the four aspects of emotional intelligence does not mean that you cannot improve the other aspects. Wanting to be aware of how emotional intelligence works is commendable and there are definitely skills and exercises that you can do to improve each and every aspect of your emotional intelligence core.

Yet, emotional intelligence can have a dark side. There are some people who are master manipulators. They are so good at emotional intelligence that they can draw upon what someone else is feeling in order to get the outcome that they want. These people know how to pit people against each other, play the victim, and play on people's emotions to remain in control at all times. If you are not emotionally intelligent, you can really fall victim to their traps rather quickly. One of the most important reasons for developing your emotional intelligence is to be a better person and to protect yourself against people who have nefarious intentions.

Lucky for Valerie, she is starting with a blank slate when learning how to develop her emotional intelligence. She does not have to be concerned about all the baggage that comes with learning a new skill. For her, she has to begin by learning what emotional intelligence is. So buckle up. The next chapter will go into more detail about how emotional intelligence affects our daily life whether we are aware of it or not.

Chapter Highlights

- Emotional intelligence was coined by Daniel Goleman in 1995 by his book *Emotional Intelligence: Why It Is More Important Than Your IQ*.
- Emotional Intelligence is composed of four different parts — self-management, self-awareness, social awareness, and relationship management.
- Our brain is composed of three regions that control our thoughts and emotions. By doing exercises to improve every aspect of our brain, one can improve their emotional intelligence.

Do the Work

Emotional Intelligence

- Why are you interested in learning more about emotional intelligence? Is it to improve personally or is it to improve in a professional setting or is it another reason? Knowing why you want to learn about emotional intelligence can help you when you get to a difficult spot in your learning.
- Do you think that you have more traits of being emotionally intelligent or more traits of not being emotionally intelligent?
- Emotional intelligence is composed of four different components — self-awareness, self-management, social awareness, and relationship management. Which component do you think you need to work on?
- Before emotional intelligence was brought to the forefront, there was a philosopher who said that "emotions are at the base of every decision?" Who was it?

Chapter 2: Emotional Intelligence in Daily Life

Remember Valerie? Yeah, things have not been going as smoothly for her ever since she's gotten home from the hospital. She has relearned basic traits such as eating and going to the restroom, but she has not discovered how to completely control her emotions yet. Her therapist keeps telling her that she needs to look into it, but she has no idea where to begin. The more she learned, she discovered that emotional intelligence is way more important in her life than she expected. Just like Valerie, emotional intelligence has a place in every person's life. However, she knows that she has a long road ahead of her.

Emotional intelligence helps our relationships with others. Emotional intelligence helps us be happier with ourselves and it helps people move throughout life a whole lot easier than if they didn't have emotional intelligence. Research has evolved to show that emotional intelligence has a place in every aspect of our life as well from the workplace to your mental and physical health to your family and social environment. While there are specific ways to improve one's emotional intelligence by focusing on the component of emotional intelligence that they are not as healthy in, there are a few general suggestions to help one improve their emotional intelligence.

One major suggestion is to expand the vocabulary that describes your emotions. When you say someone is happy, what version of happy are they? Are they ecstatic, mellow, or jumping with joy? When someone is mad, are they livid, disappointed, or upset? If you need help developing your emotional vocabulary, you can start by learning a new emotional word daily by going to the dictionary. You can even learn foreign words to help with your task. The more vocabulary you have to describe how you are feeling and how others are feeling helps your brain react to emotional situations better.

Emotional intelligence can be tricky because a person can hide the emotions that they are feeling. If you expect all people to cry when they are sad, a person who is sad and does not cry and laughs instead will throw you off guard. How about if a person is happy and cries for joy instead of smiling and laughing when they are happy? People who react to their emotions in a non-stereotypical way can cause you issues when trying to figure out how to react to their emotions. On the other hand, there are tons of people who are pros at hiding their true emotions. Someone can be boiling on the inside, but outwardly say that they are happy. If people are able to lie about how they feel or act in ways that always truly depict how they feel, how in the world are you able to determine the best response of responding to people?

Research points to a new way of understanding how our brain works which in turn will help us understand how to be better at being emotionally intelligent. We already know that our brain has three different parts that help determine your emotions and controls how to react to your emotions and the emotional responses of others. Researchers have now figured out that our brain works from an encyclopedia of experiences that we have. The more information we have in our brain's encyclopedia and the varied emotions we can draw from, the better reactions our brain can pull out from its encyclopedia of emotional responses in order to determine what is the best way to react to any given situation. (This is why understanding the different degrees of emotions by improving your emotional vocabulary are important.) Research has helped us to understand that even though people sometimes say one thing, their face gives away their true emotions. Maybe they are smiling but they have a slight scowl which points to their true displeasure. Maybe they are smiling but their eyes have sadness about them or their smile doesn't include their eyes. Understanding the nuances of emotions helps someone draw quickly and correctly from their brain's encyclopedia. This ability to break down emotions and their nuances are called emotional granularity. This is an important tool to have in your emotional intelligence toolkit.

Self-awareness is an important aspect of emotional intelligence in our day-to-day living. Since emotional intelligence is layered, this would be the first layer to master. Self-aware people are able to identify and understand their emotions quickly. A key benefit of being self-aware is knowing when you are engaging in toxic behavior or even engaging in overly happy behavior that can cause issues as well. When they are able to identify these emotions, then they are able to properly choose how to manage those emotions. For example, stress is a common issue that many people have to deal with. Research has shown that stress is a common denominator in certain chronic illness like heart diseases, high blood pressure, and obesity to name a few. However, emotionally intelligent people are able to deal with it easier and sustain themselves in stressful situations in a way that people who are not emotionally intelligent are unable to. For example, an emotionally intelligent person is able to quickly identify what stresses them out and then choose the proper response to that trigger. This is what self-management is. Knowing how to respond to any given situation and it is the second layer of emotional intelligence. When you are emotionally intelligent, you are able to properly de-escalate the situation when you are feeling stressed whether that is to alter your surroundings or properly handle your responses to other people. In some instances, stress is unavoidable especially if certain relationships you have bring on stress. Emotionally intelligent people find amazing ways to handle the stress to prevent a mental health breakdown. At times, a professional must be sought when dealing with stress and its impact on your life. That's totally ok. The key to being self-aware is the action part of the definition when you decide to do something about the emotions you are facing. (Remember, non-action is also a form of action.) Many people can identify issues they may have, but choose to do nothing about it or continue in the same destructive cycles. Self-aware people and those who practice self-management are able to manage the situation and come out stronger than before.

For Valerie, to improve her emotional intelligence, she has to rebuild her emotional encyclopedia so she has experiences to draw from. After the wreck, she spent lots of time at home recovering. She got to learn her family better and engaged with many health professionals that helped with her recovery. She also discovered Google which is an amazing tool that she has been using to develop her emotional intelligence. During this time, she was able to learn what types of things that made her happy and what made her upset. She noticed that having breakfast in bed delivered to her made her happy. She noticed that when her children did what she wanted them to do, that made her happy. On the other side, when the nurses made her take medicine she did not want, she did not like it. Initially, she realized that throwing a tantrum like a toddler did not help. She had to manage the emotion in a different way. She realized that she could express her displeasure in a different way. She could state that she did not like taking the medication, but would still take it. The key to remember from this example is that communication is the key when you are managing the emotions that you may have. Oftentimes, identifying the emotion is the easy part. The difficult part of being emotionally intelligent happens when you have to manage those emotions. And for many people, communication is especially difficult when you have to explain unpleasant things to people. However, emotionally intelligent person expressed how they feel and then take the action. Valerie realized that while she did not like taking her medicine, she would have to in order to get well. So the response she deemed appropriate to this situation was to express her displeasure while taking the medicine since it was necessary.

Social awareness is the next aspect of emotional intelligence that affects us in our day-to-day life. It is the third layer to master. The social setting in which you find yourself plays a role in how you handle

Emotional Intelligence

yourself. You know the saying, "There's a time and place for everything?" It is true. Social awareness is summed up neatly in that saying. A person is going to act differently at home than they would at work versus how they would act in a religious setting or a social setting like a bar or club. To master social awareness, you have to pick up quickly on what type of setting you are in. Is it formal or more relaxed? Is it professional or is it casual? One way to figure that out if you have no idea is to look at what other people are doing. How are they dressed? Are they wearing skimpy clothes or suits and dresses? How are they talking? Are they talking loudly, normally, or are they being quiet? What kind of language are they using? Are they using profanity or are they using vernacular or academic language? To understand how to act properly, you can also look at how others are acting in the situation. Are they being loud? Or only a few people are being loud? Then notice how other people are reacting to them. Noticing how people act and how others react to their actions is a big clue on how to be socially aware. Are people who wear certain clothes acting a certain way or are they being outcasted? The key to mastering being socially aware is to become observant and notice what is going on around you. A trick that some people use no matter what social setting they are in is to be quiet, sit in a corner and watch what is going on. Socially aware people sometimes take people that they trust to the side to ask questions about social settings they may find themselves in. On the flip side, you have to be true in situations no matter what others are doing, even if it is deemed socially acceptable. For example, have you ever found yourself in a situation where it was ok to bully and make fun of other people? That's not a nice thing, but if you don't bully the other person, then people would be bullying you. Emotionally intelligent people are able to stand for their beliefs even when it is unfavorable.

Valerie had to quickly realize that social settings dictate her reactions. After taking the medicine she did not like, she has been approved to go back to her former job. She works as a customer service representative at a technology company that manufactures the latest software. Before she was involved in her accident, she was a top customer service rep. After going through a two-week training, her love for technology has come back. She is a pro at understanding the technology, but understanding how to deal with other people in a work setting is proving to be a challenge. First, Valerie has to deal with the customers. Next, she has to deal with her co-workers and then she has to deal with her managers and supervisors. She notices that the company is pretty relaxed. She does not have to dress up for work. Valerie is able to pick up on the playful banter amongst her co-workers and managers that make her feel more relaxed. The company also plays music in the background to help deal with the stress.

Everything was going well until Valerie has to deal with a very angry customer on a call. Flabbergasted, she is immediately quiet. She notices that the person right beside her seems to be on a stressful call and they are biting the top of their pen vigorously. Valerie has no idea how to respond. Her initial thought is to yell at the customer and hang up, but last week, she saw someone do that and that co-worker lost their job. The longer she waits on how to respond to the customer, she notices that the person's voice continues to rise. Valerie feels her heartbeat racing and she knows that getting yelled at is a stress trigger of hers. She looks around and notices that her co-worker begins to smile and talk with their difficult customer so she thinks she will try that. Valerie begins to smile and notices immediately that her heartbeat slows down. She talks slowly and begins to give the customer options on how to resolve the conflict. She notices that her co-workers are doing similar techniques. She begins to relax and the customer decides that she would like to speak with a manager. Valerie immediately transfers the call to a manager. Valerie was able to handle her social setting by observing what others were doing and making notes of examples of what she had seen before. In this came, the old adage "When in Rome, do as the Romans do" saved her. After that one incident, Valerie was able to continue being relaxed, yet professional in her work setting.

Relationship management is the last key component that we have to deal with in our daily life and it is the last component of emotional intelligence. Relationships are everywhere! Our relationship with our self is of utmost importance, but our relationships with others are just as important. Emotionally intelligent people know how to react to a situation based on the relationship they have with someone. A relationship with a homeless stranger on the street will be different from your spouse versus the relationship with your teenager or toddler. Knowing the dynamics of every relationship is very important. Most people have a baseline of respect and kindness for everyone they meet. This could also be described as common courtesy. But emotionally intelligent people understand the nuances of relationships, and when necessary, they can manipulate a relationship to get the results that they want. In this case, manipulation is not being defined as a negative, but as an action that emotionally intelligent people know how to use to navigate situations in their daily life. People who use manipulation to control people for nefarious gains are different from people who use manipulation to get the results that they want. Evil manipulators tend to cause destruction in their relationships, whereas, emotionally intelligent people are able to maintain their relationships and they are able to return the favor of scratching others back when necessary.

An often understated, important aspect of being an emotionally intelligent being is the importance of knowing how to manage your time. Time-management is a crucial foundation that emotional intelligence rests on. Have you ever noticed how calm people who always have it together seem to be? They do not ever seem frazzled and their hair always seems to be done? Well, time management is a tool I'm sure they are using. Just like emotional intelligence, time management is a skill that can be learned. Later on in the book, we will take a look at how important time management is and work on an activity to evaluate your time management.

Our friend Valerie is noticing that there is a difference in the way that her co-workers treat her versus her husband and her children. One thing she has noticed is that they know how to manage their situation to get optimal results. As a working mom, she is having a difficult time managing her responsibilities at home. On one hand, she has to handle her responsibilities at her job and on the other hand, she has to handle her cooking, cleaning, and personal maintenance too. She feels like there is not enough time in the day. She feels like her mind is racing all the time and she is having small panic attacks. She has no idea what to do except to ask for help from the different relationships that she has.

Valerie first had a sit down with her husband to see if he wouldn't mind ordering take out or preparing food for the kids once or twice a week to see if she could get some me time. Because Valerie quickly realized that the best time to ask her husband about something is after she serves him her famous lemon meringue pie, she asked him right after he ate a piece. Of course, he happily agreed. The next task she knew she needed to accomplish was to get her children, a teenager and toddler, to take more responsibility in the household. Instead of whining to her children, she knew the dynamics of the relationship and she was able to use humor to address the issue. Her children happily agreed. The stress from trying to do everything herself had begun to pack on the pounds. So she began to meditate, exercise, communicate better, and clear out her schedule. Valerie realized that reaching out to the relationships that she had and communicating her feelings and how they can make the best out of the relationship was important. Valerie felt super accomplished!

Things were going well for a week until everything went back to the way they were. Valerie no longer had time to exercise or relax. She went back to scrambling to do everything. One night, she hears a ring at the doorbell. It is Patty, the interim replacement to her neighborhood association who wanted to know when Valerie could take her position back. Valerie has a tumble of emotions and she is not sure how to react so she told Patty she would think about it.

As you can see, Valerie thought that she had everything figured out, but soon learned that the journey to emotional intelligence is never over. You are always learning and developing your emotional intelligence. Some days are better than others and some days are total, utter failures. Valerie's life feels quite chaotic again and she needs the tools of emotional intelligence to learn how to navigate. In order to do so, she must first learn how to be in touch with her emotions. She must learn how to thoroughly dissect what her emotions mean and that is the subject of the next chapter of the book.

Chapter Highlights

- Emotional granularity is paramount in helping you pick out a wide range of emotions to choose from. The wider your emotional vocabulary, whether the words come from foreign languages or your native language, the better you are able to create an encyclopedia in which your brain can draw from when trying to figure out what is the proper reaction to any situation.
- There are different tools you can use to prepare yourself with emotional intelligence such as meditation, exercise, and communication.
- Self-awareness, self-management, social awareness, and relationship all play a major role in our day-to-day life.

Do the Work

Emotional Intelligence

- Make a commitment to find words to describe emotional situations that you find yourself in. Try to pepper your language with a few foreign words to give your emotional vocabulary and encyclopedia more nuance.
- How would you rate your level of communication on a scale of 1 to 10? Be honest with yourself.
- What are some initial thoughts you have on how you can improve your communication?
- How are you currently handling your time management? Is there anything you can get rid of?
- If you were Valerie, what would be your initial response when speaking with Patty? What do you think would be the best response for responding to Patty?

Chapter 3: Building Self-Awareness Skills

Valerie often has weird sensations. She has learned that these weird sensations are called emotions. She has developed a basic emotional intelligence encyclopedia to include words like happy, sad, flabbergasted, upset – you know the basics. Up until this point, she thinks that she is pretty ok despite being in a devastating accident. She notices that sometimes people see her and they tend to go in the opposite direction. She is normally loud. She's never heard of the word filter, so she just says what is on her mind. She also makes jokes that aren't funny and laughs hysterically at them not understanding that sometimes the things she says may be offensive in nature. She tries to be nice to people, but no one seems to want to be around her. She isn't sure why. That's when she has learned about being self-aware, the first component of self-awareness.

Self-awareness is the master key to unlocking emotional intelligence. Once you have a deeper understanding of what self-awareness is and go about becoming self-aware, the rest of the components of emotional intelligence becomes easier. Being self-aware is difficult. That's why lots of people avoid being self-aware. They delude themselves into thinking they are perfect because that's easier than facing the cold hard truth about themselves. Do not be like those people. I want to commend you, number one, for picking up this book, it shows that you are open to having an honest conversation with yourself. What should a conversation with yourself about being self-aware look like? What questions would you need to ask yourself? This chapter will help you have that conversation and start on the path of self-awareness. The first section is all about knowing yourself and the second is about how to motivate yourself to become the person you want to be.

Self-awareness is important, yet difficult because it is all about examining your actions. You have to look at your past behaviors and your present behavior to understand how you can change your actions. Self-awareness is also difficult because we tend to be biased about our actions. Let's face it. We think we are the greatest thing. Do not get me wrong. It is great to have self-esteem about who we are, but it is more important to be realistic about our opportunities for improvement in order to carve out the best life possible for ourselves. Being self-aware brings on a bevy of benefits. When you are self-aware, you are able to be more empathetic and compassionate to everyone that you meet instead of just being blinded by your ignorance and personal biases. Self-aware people are able to relate to a variety of people because they are open-minded and able to adjust their emotions to someone despite their own inherent biases and prejudices. Self-aware people do have biases, but they are able to identify those biases. Self-aware people are not blindsided by their prejudices to the point where they can't understand where the feeling they may have is coming from. Self-aware people know their strengths and weaknesses and are open-minded and fair. However, they do not get this way unless they have a heart-to-heart with themselves.

The first thing you need to do before you have this conversation is to set aside a day for yourself. Make sure that you will not be interrupted because this will be one of the most difficult conversations that you will have. You can bring tissue, pen, and paper. You can have your computer nearby if necessary to keep notes digitally. You can also buy a journal if you prefer to keep notes by hand without having to deal with individual pieces of paper. You can even have an empowering music playlist because you may need it. Give permission to yourself to feel every emotion that you may experience with no judgment then go ahead and buckle your proverbial seat-belt. There are no other people who can have this conversation with you.

Emotional Intelligence

The first topic of discussion you want to have with yourself is figuring out what personality type you are. There are lots of personality online assessments that are free, easy, and quick to take that gives you an insight about your personality. On the piece of paper, what are your initial thoughts of who you are? Are you hot-tempered? Are you level-headed and cool or are you a mixture of both? Whatever you are, think about it and then take an assessment test. One of the most popular personality tests is the Jung and Briggs Myers typology test or the Predictive Index. However, there are other ones that you can try out if you prefer.

After taking the test, you will next want to ask yourself a series of questions:

- Who is the person that you admire the most? What is it that you admire about them?
- What character traits do you love about yourself? This does not have to be related to emotional intelligence. It can be something that makes you feel great about yourself.
- What character traits do you love about others? What are those traits that you wish you had?
- What do you consider your core values to be? Think about these values from a spiritual, emotional, mental, physical, and financial perspective.
- Who is the person you want to be? Think about the legacy you want to leave. Who will people say that you were when you leave this world?
- What do you think your purpose in life is? For some people, this consists of who you want to help and how you want to help them. They take into account what activities they like to do and activities they do not like to do when making this decision.
- How would you rate your self-esteem on a scale of 1-10, with 10 being the highest?

Emotional Intelligence

- How are you working on your self-esteem? What daily habits are you forming to make sure that your self-esteem is high and you will not be susceptible to bad decisions?
- Are you working on becoming that person daily?
- What are your strengths? What things are easy for you and what things do other people say you are good at?
- What are your weaknesses? In other words, what are areas that you can improve upon? Weaknesses are also known as areas or opportunities.
- What daily habits are making your weaknesses worse?
- What daily habits are improving your strengths?
- How would your closest friends and family members describe you?
- Do people, especially your friends and family, typically tell you the truth or what you want to hear? Do they think you are sensitive and tend to hedge how they tell you the truth? Or are they very blunt with you and are not afraid to hurt your feelings if you need to know the truth?
- On a scale of 1 to 10, how would you describe your communication skills? Why would you describe it that way? Give three examples.
- On a scale of 1 to 10, how do you describe your communication skills when you are angry, stressed, or arguing? Give three examples of why you feel that way.
- When do you typically analyze your successful day or successful days to see why they were successful? If you do not, come up with a time when you should start doing that.
- What do you do when you accomplish your goals or are happy? Does your celebratory behavior turn into negative habits?
- When do you typically analyze your horrible days and failures to see why it went wrong and what you can do to improve it?
- How often do you seek out constructive criticism that can help you improve? Who do you go to when you need to get

constructive criticism? If you don't have anyone, who could you go to?
- What is your spiritual outlook in life? Go more into detail. What are your views about the afterlife?
- What do you feel when someone you know is successful? Are you generally happy for them or do you tend to get jealous? Think about the why behind your behavior. This will help you develop more trends.
- What do you feel when someone you know fails? Are you happy with glee? Do you feel like you are in a competition with them?

Once you go through all of these questions, a conversation you would like to have is with someone you trust. Ask them do they agree with the results of the personality test and with the answers to the above questions that you asked yourself. The trick is to ask someone who will be honest with you, yet tactful and constructive. You may be surprised that the way you value or think about yourself is not how other people look at you at all. Be sure to take what they say with a grain of salt because they have their bias as well. When you are listening to other people, do not get defensive. Be quiet. The only thing you should say to them is thank you. Combining your personality assessment results plus feedback from other people plus what your thoughts are will be able to get a clearer view if you are the person that you think you are.

The next conversation you need to have with yourself is to figure out what types of things make you upset. On your piece of paper, draw four lines to create 5 columns. At the top of the first column, write triggers. At the top of the second column, write reactions. At the top of the third column, write 'How Do I Feel?' At the top of the fourth column, write 'How Would I Like to React?' Then on the last column, write 'Steps I'm Taking.' Then brainstorm. What things push your buttons? Is it when somebody chews with their mouth open? Is it when someone pops their gum? Is it when someone tells you directions from the passenger seat? Whatever the trigger that upsets you, write it down on the left side.

Questions you can consider when thinking about your reactions:

- Do you blow up? Do you tend to yell and scream or say bad words?
- Do you just ignore what is bothering you until you blow up? Do you avoid expressing how you feel and find yourself blowing up before it's too late?
- Are you able to address the issue constructively? Are you able to be calm and solution-focused?
- How do you feel about your normal reaction?
- Do you think it is getting the job done or do you find yourself still frustrated?
- When you try to confront someone about the situation, are you doing it gracefully or are you being confrontational? Do you yell and scream or do you find that you are normally calm?

Now that you know what your trigger is and how you typically react, how would you like to react? Would you like to be more graceful? Would you like to ignore insignificant things that bother you? Once you add that, consider how you feel about these reactions. Do you think there is work you can do on your reactions? Do you feel like you are doing ok? Lastly, figure out a way to better manage your reactions by the expectations that you would. By knowing what your triggers are, you can better handle how you react to those things. This type of deep reflection is an important way for you to become more self-aware. It also helps you create a stress-management system to handle things that may stress you out. What are you going to do when you are stressed? Take the time to create that system now so you are effectively handling your stress.

Emotional Intelligence

If you've made it this far, great job! We have more introspecting to do, so go ahead and buckle your seatbelt. This is where things can get ugly. The nature of being self-aware is one of introspection and honesty even when it is uncomfortable. You have to take an intense look into your past in order to figure out where you're going in the future. So now we are going to take a deep look into your past.

The first thing you want to consider is what are the very best memories you have from your earliest memory to the present time? Then think about what are the very worst memories that you have from the earliest memory to the present time? Please take your time when writing these memories down and go in as much detail as possible. This is essentially a written record of who you are. Next, you need to think about the conclusions that you drew from those memories? What are the results and conclusions that you have from those memories of life? Do these conclusions help you make judgments about people or about life in general? For example, if you had a cousin that only kept tootsie rolls and threw all other lollipops out, does that affect why you only like tootsie rolls now? Do you think Tootsie Roll lollipops are horrible without ever having a Tootsie Roll lollipop yourself so you are unable to conclusively make a judgment about whether you like Tootsie Roll lollipops or not?

After you have your memories down and the conclusions you've gained from those memories, now you have to dig deeper. It is time to make two columns. Title this page 'My Beliefs.' At the top of the left column, write 'Healthy Beliefs.' At the top of the right column, write 'Limiting Beliefs.' Next review the list of conclusions from your memories and put the appropriate belief in the proper corresponding column. Which ones are healthy? Which ones are limiting you?

A limiting belief is a belief that is not necessarily true, but one that you believe based on experiences that have shaped your views. An example of a limiting belief would be that if you need to get healthy, but you see that no one in your family is healthy, you may believe that being healthy is not a big deal since no one in your family takes health seriously. Thus, you feel that being healthy is underrated and this limiting belief hinders you from seeking a healthier lifestyle. Limiting beliefs do not have to be just about negative beliefs. Sometimes limiting beliefs can be positive, but also hinder you. For example, lots of people have the limiting belief that 'The love of money is the root of all evil' which in turn causes them to have negative thoughts about money. They think if they make a lot of money, they will be evil so they do not seek out opportunities to make money which in turn would improve their life. Even though it is good advice that loving money too much can be evil, it is a limiting belief when taking it out of context and hindering one's growth.

As you examine your memories, ask yourself questions about these memories:

- Did we play a role in any of these memories? Do we need to take responsibility for any of these actions? Try to look at the situation objectively like you are a bird viewing the situation from a bird's eye point-of-view
- Can you fill any personal needs without destructive behavior? You can do everything in moderation. But are you doing anything in excess?
- Are you living for today or are you stuck in the past trying to fix any of these memories? Sometimes the past can weigh us down. It is good to see the past as a way to enlighten your future behaviors but not to the point of your past limiting your future happiness.
- Is there anything that you can improve to proactively handle any of these situations in the future? If you notice any negative trends or cycles from your memories, how can you stop them and turn those negative cycles into positive cycles?

- Do I need to step out my comfort zone? Am I stuck in my ways? Do I need to eat at new restaurants, be around different people or travel some to open myself up to new experiences? When you go to the restaurant, do you order the same thing every single time? This one should be pretty easy to answer, but another big clue if people tell you that you are stuck in your ways.

While examining the conclusions you may have about your memories, you may also realize that you have some forgiving and forgetting to do. You may need to call someone and ask them for their forgiveness. No matter how big or small, make note of the trends you see in your conclusions and be honest with yourself about how these memories are affecting you now. Be mindful that if you need to speak to someone and they are not receptive of your experience, that's ok. Say what you need to say and move on. Try your hardest to make peace with the painful memories. In the midst of this activity, you may also realize that you need to set boundaries. Boundaries are important because they help you figure out how to handle people. If you know that certain people are not good, make a boundary to not be around them. If you know that during a certain time of the month, certain things piss you off more than other things, set yourself up for success and create the necessary hedges around you. At this point, if you notice you may want to talk to a therapist to do more work on these memories, do not hesitate to find one and set an appointment.

Doing this activity may stir up lots of emotions and that's okay. If at any point you need to take a step back, feel free to do so. Then come back. The most important thing to remember is that your emotions or feelings are important. They are how you feel about a particular situation. Be kind to yourself and be non-judgmental about these feelings.

Emotional Intelligence

This next section is all about how to become self-motivated and become the person you want to be. Self-aware people know who they are and the person they want to become. To start on this journey of being self-motivated, we have more work to do.

The next things we need to consider are your daily activities. Please keep track of your daily activities in your journal. You can print off an online schedule and fill it in if you need to. When you're filling in your schedule, make sure that you are tracking your energy levels, sleep patterns, and what you're eating as well. Questions you can ask would be:

- What time of day are you doing your best work? Think about when you are most productive. What other factors do you notice contribute to your productivity? Is it when you have peace and quiet and your kids are not around or is it when it is loud and chaos are around you. This is specific to your personality.
- Is this time consistent or does it change? Another great trend to notice when answering this question is to think about the moon. Are you most productive when it is a full moon or at another time?
- What time of the day are you not doing your best work? Knowing when you are not productive will help you to not schedule productive activities during that time. For some people who are morning owls, any time in the night does not work them. For others, the afternoons just do not work and other people prefer to be midnight owl.
- Is this time the same or does it change?
- What activities are draining you during the day? Do you exercise or hang out with exhausting people? Think of all the things that tend to deplete your energy levels.
- What activities are giving me energy? Do you notice if you have a certain schedule that it gives you energy? Do you notice

that it helps when you are around other people who do not procrastinate? Make an exhaustive list.
- Do you notice any difference in your energy levels depending on the foods you eat? Do you have more energy when you only eat certain foods? Do caffeine and sugar cause you to crash often? Does meat cause your stomach to hurt? Does eating a heavy lunch fuel you for the rest of the day?
- Are you getting enough sleep daily? For most people, 8 hours is recommended, but other can get ways with anything from 5-7 hours. When do you notice that you are most productive?
- Are you happy most days? Or are you miserable most days? How would you say that you feel generally? Do you feel that you are living in your purpose?

The next thing you want to consider is your daily habits that are building self-awareness? Are you meditating or journaling? If not, it is something you definitely want to consider whether you are doing these activities digitally with an app or with old-school methods like a journal, pen, and paper.

An easy template to use when reflecting on your days and helps you stay focused on being the person you want to be includes five simple questions:

- Did I learn anything to do? If so, what? Try to be as detailed as possible.
- Did anything go bad today? If so, what? Try to be as detailed as possible.
- What did I do nicely for myself today? Did you say kind words to yourself for doing a job well done or anything that would boost your self-esteem?
- What went great today? What things did you do really well today?

- Is there anything I can do to make tomorrow better than today? Be specific and list a way that you can make tomorrow better than today. If the day was a phenomenal day, you can write ways you can make the next day just as good as today.

You should also consider whether you should start meditating or journaling. To begin journaling, find a journal and just freely write about everything that bothers you. By doing the work of free writing, you are able to write about anything that's bothering you. You are in charge of your destiny. The great thing about journaling is that you have a record of your emotions. You can notice patterns and trends in your behavior to see what makes you anxious, depressed, or happy.

Meditation is another form of being self-aware. To meditate, find a nice cozy place that's yours and yours alone. Set aside a few minutes of your time every day to journal or to meditate. You want to practice breathing deeply from your diaphragm and let your thoughts gently go by. You will find that your mind and your body open up and will improve. Self-awareness is hard but necessary.

For Valerie, she thinks that she is getting the hang of what it means to be self-aware. She is becoming more aware of how others are perceiving her and has begun to try and develop a way to be more culturally sensitive. She has also laid off saying all the bad words that express her displeasure and the corny insensitive jokes. She has a limited past to work with that explains how she acts the way she acts. In her case, she is learning a lot of her behaviors from the television, especially reality TV, but she has come to the conclusion that the television is not how reality works. Thankfully, her husband and children have been patient with her throughout this entire ideal and have patiently worked with her to explain why certain things are appropriate for her to say and why other things are not ideal. She has been learning rapidly but still has lots of more learning to go. As she continues to be self-aware of her actions and how she carries herself, she notices that people want to come around her a lot more than they did before. Yet, she tends to have random bouts of not knowing how to handle the intensity of emotions that she is feeling. The next chapter will focus on how to manage our emotions now that we are more tuned with them.

Chapter Highlights

- Self-awareness is all about being in tune with your emotions. A major part of becoming self-aware is uncovering feelings from the past to determine how those feelings affect in the future. Once you do that, you are able to work on your self-esteem and figure out ways to handle your emotions.
- Asking questions about who you are and analyzing your past experiences can be a long process, but they are very helpful in helping you figure out how to be self-aware. This step helps you to figure out trends that are informing your current behavior and can provide insight on how to become the person that you want to be.
- When you are self-aware, you're able to live in the moment. Practices that help you be more aware include meditation and journaling about your experiences.

Do the Work

- What are some questions that you can ask yourself when you're being honest about yourself that was not mentioned?
- Who are some people that you do not admire? How can you avoid being like them?
- What practices are you going to incorporate into your life in order to become more self-aware?
- What time will you set aside to do the work of answering the questions about who you are and looking at your past experiences?

Emotional Intelligence

Here are some helpful scenarios that can help you with your self-awareness. This helps you to think through ways to be aware of your emotions and apply the concepts learned in this chapter. There is no right or wrong answer. You can take this practice to the next level by role-playing with friends.

1. You notice that every time you talk about someone to your spouse, they immediately began to act testy with you. You do not understand why since you are only complimenting the person and expressing how awesome the person is. How should you react?

    A. You should tell them to get over it. They do not have to act like a wet rug just because you give someone else a compliment. You are not in charge of their behavior.

    B. You can ask them why they act like that every time you bring up this person's name. Give them your assumptions about why they act like that in order to break the ice.

    C. You can bring the person over for dinner and then see if your spouse acts the same way in front of them. If they do, then ask them both to resolve whatever issues they may be having.

    D. You can just avoid talking about the person around your spouse and keep your thoughts to yourself. If they are acting this way, this must mean that they are comfortable and you want to treat others the way you want to be treated.

2. There is a painful memory that you cannot seem to get over. You know that this memory is affecting your current behavior and you want to find a way to deal with it effectively. The person who is the source of this memory will be in town soon. How should you handle the situation?

Emotional Intelligence

    A. You should write a letter and hand deliver it to the person. Then officially let the pain go once the letter is delivered. You can follow-up to see what their thoughts are about the letter.

    B. You should invite them to dinner and explain the issue you have and try to seek a resolution. If they are not receptive to what you have to say, you can move forward without gaining any closure.

    C. You should ask them to meet you at a boxing ring and fight it out. Sometimes letting your pain out physically is the best way.

    D. You shouldn't say anything. You should reach out to a therapist and get them to help you figure the problem out.

3. There is someone who is constantly talking about your weight. You already know that you can stand to lose a few pounds, but every time you see this person, they remind you in a non-constructive way and it makes you uncomfortable. What is the best way to handle this situation?

    A. The next time they say something, sock them in the mouth. They need to learn a lesson, specifically how not to be so insensitive.

    B. Let them know that you do not like what they are doing. And if they keep doing it, then sock them in the face.

    C. Avoid this person. If this person comes around, give them the silent treatment so you do not have to deal with them. Do not ruin your mood to be around people you do not like. The feeling is probably mutual.

    D. Communicate with this person and let them know that what they are doing makes you uncomfortable and then request that

Emotional Intelligence

they stop. If they do not, let them know that you will no longer seek to be around them.

4. You have discovered a limiting belief that you have. You are currently working on overcoming this limiting belief and have done quite well. However, you had a relapse and you are not sure if you can correct the behavior that your relapse has caused. What should you do?

   A. You should continue to work on overcoming this limiting belief. It took you a lifetime to develop this limiting belief so you shouldn't expect it to go away overnight.

   B. Mope and pout. If the damage is irreversible, just accept the damage and move forward. Having a pity party is sometimes the best, soul-cleansing solution.

   C. Try to be proactive and correct the damage that has been caused. Then continue to work on overcoming your limiting belief.

   D. Do not do anything. See how the cards may fall and then go from there. Sometimes we expect the worse and the situation is not as bad as we imagine it.

5. You have taken a personality test, but you do not agree with the results. You take another one and the results seem more accurate, how should you interpret the results?

   A. You should ignore them. These things aren't true at all. There is a certain percentage that it may not be true so do not feel bad.

   B. You should take another personality test and then see what it says before you make your conclusion. Two is better than one.

C. You should take the tests results as the truth. Sometimes we behave in ways that we are not self-aware enough to recognize as the truth.

D. Take the results with a grain of salt and ask someone you trust if they agree with the results or not.

Chapter 4: Building Self-Management Skills

Valerie has had great days and bad days. One trend she notices is that she never knows how to act when she experiences emotions. When she's happy, she tends to leap for joy, shout, and dance. When she's sad, she normally cries hysterically until someone asks her what is wrong. Then she can explain what is going on. When she's angry, she yells, screams, and breaks things. Everyone tends to cower and run away in fear. In other words, she typically goes with her base instincts and lets the card fall as they may. However, after studying emotional intelligence, she knows there has to be another way. After doing the work in chapter 3 to figure out her current emotions, without the ability to explore her past memories (thanks amnesia!), Valerie is ready to move forward with learning how to manage her emotions.

This chapter is all about looking into the emotional intelligence toolbox and pulling out the skill of self-management. Self-management is all about how you control your emotions after you recognize what those emotions are. Self-management is crucial in knowing when exactly to use the emotions that you have. Self-management is important to know that when dealing with a sensitive person to not to break them loudly or in front of a group of people. Self-management is knowing that having an attention tantrum in the middle of a store is not the appropriate time or place to handle your complaints. When you know how to manage yourself, you have tackled an important aspect of emotional intelligence. Each component of self-management works together to help you improve yourself management skill set. Self-management consists of four different components. They are consists of your initiative, having a positive outlook, a focus on your physical health and your emotional healing, and how you are able to breathe and relax.

The first key to improving your self-management is to fine-tune your outlook in life. Do you normally have a positive or negative outlook? You need to decide that you are going to be kind to yourself. If you usually beat yourself down, today is the day that you stop it. If you are one that generally has positive self-talk, we're going to take it up another level. Right now, make a decision that you are going to be kind to yourself and you're going to work on being the person that you want to be. Repeat after me 'I am a wonderful person and I am going to be the person that I want to be.' Because you have made a commitment to yourself, you have no choice but to accomplish. If you want to take this commitment to another level, you can even write yourself a special contract. Write a mission statement on the type of person you want to be, date it, and sign your name. You can also hang it up in a special place so you can look at it and know that you have made a commitment to yourself to be a better person than what you have been.

People who are emotionally intelligent usually are go-getters. So if you're not a go-getter, how do you become one? That's easy — you put in the work. You must first try to understand what the vision is for your life. Are you comfortable and secure in yourself? If not, you may want to try a few different exercises to help you figure out where you're going in life.

The first exercise is called 'Write Your Autobiography/ Obituary.' And it is just as the title states. When you go down in the history books, how do you want people to remember you? You can create this legacy by writing your autobiography or your obituary. Take a few seconds to write it down. There are many items that can be included.

- Where did you go to school? Where did you go for elementary, middle, secondary school or graduate school?
- What career did you pursue? Did you jump around in your professional life or did you stick to one profession?

- Do you feel like you were able to follow your life's passion? Did you feel like you were able to follow your life's calling?
- Who did you become? Did you receive any great accolades?
- What family did you leave behind? Were you married? Did you have any children?
- How would your enemies view you? How would your friends view you?
- How did you raise your children? Where they raised completely different than you or similarly?
- Did you have any pets?
- What do you consider your greatest legacy to be? It can be something you are famous for or something that you are not famous for.
- Would you be famous or make an impact on the people that you love?
- Where would you hold your funeral? Would it be in a church or elsewhere? What country or city would it be held in?

After you write it, take a silent moment and see if you're on track to fulfilling what you want to do. If you feel okay about the progress you've made so far, great! However, if you feel like you're unsettled and you are not accomplishing what you want to accomplish, that's also good. Now you have the opportunity to take the necessary steps to turn your life around and begin to live the life that you want to live. Being a go-getter is an important part of self-management and the only person in charge of changing your life is you. If you want to be emotionally intelligent, decide to live the life that you want to live. Do not find yourself living for someone else.

Another daily habit that will help you build self-awareness is if you are noticing and improving your self-talk. We talk to ourselves all the time. If we are saying positive things to ourselves, it makes a difference compared to when we are saying negative things. People who are highly emotionally intelligent use positive self-talk across to themselves. When the chips are down, they are speaking life to themselves. They are not using words like 'I can't,' 'I will not,' or 'I am not able to do that.' They use powerful words such as 'I will,' 'I can,' 'I am able to,' and 'I am going to.' Take a quick moment to think about your self-talk. When you speak to yourself, is it negative or positive?

Let's do a quick exercise to help you reset your self-talk if you need to work on that. It is time for your handy-dandy journal again. This time create three columns. At the top of the left column, write positive self-talk, in the middle column, write 'Negative Self-Talk,' and at the top of the right-hand column write 'Improved Self-Talk.' Next, reflect on the language you use when talking to yourself. Are you saying 'I can…,' 'I will…' or 'I will not…,' or 'I can't…'? What phrases are you repeating to yourself? Add them to the appropriate column. Then underline the action verb of those statements. Are the underlined verbs negative or positive? Now move to the right side of that line. Create a positive version or a more positive version of yourself talk. Then underline the words The Burbs twice in this section. If you are prone to negative self-talk, replace that negative talk with those double underlined words. Next, you'll want to change those negative affirmations to positive ones so that you are saying positive words to yourself.

You can take this activity up a notch by creating affirmations. Affirmations are short motivational statements that you can create. You can add this to your column of 'Improved Self-Talk.' Affirmations are mantras that you can chant or positive words that help you think and say positive things. Reflect back on your obituary. What is something that you want to do that you are currently not doing? Create a mantra and begin repeating it in order to get to where you need to get. Take out a sheet a paper or use one in your journal. Draw a line in the middle. On the left side of the paper, write the goals that you want to do. Then on the right-hand side, write a mantra that is directly related to that goal. For example, if you say I want to be a school teacher. On the right-hand side, write 'I will be a school teacher' or 'I am taking the necessary steps to be a school teacher.'

If you need a template, you can just use a positive affirmation in front of the goal and repeat that at least twice a day. The more you repeat it, the more the affirmation will lodge into your self-conscious and you will be able to make the right decisions that will help you reach your goals.

Other affirmations you can use include:

- I am worthy.
- I will succeed.
- I am able.
- I am loved.
- I am happy.
- I can do this.
- I am great and I'm working on my greatness every day.
- I am calm and at peace.
- I am self-aware.
- I am a beautiful work in progress.

To create your own affirmations, make the affirmation positive and in the present tense. You can create the affirmations to reflect your personal goals and habits.

The next exercise you want to do is a visualization activity where you visualize great things for your future. When you visualize, you want to be as specific as possible. If you want to be a teacher, make sure that you describe what type of teacher you want to be. What type of students are you going to teach? What does your classroom look like? The more detailed you are, the better your subconscious becomes rooted. As a reinforcement to this visualization exercise, you can even create a vision board. In a safe place, put up a board with cutouts and pictures that describe your goals and your needs. Look at that every day as a reminder of what you want to do. The more you feel secure in yourself and in your goals, the better your self-management of your own emotions will be because you have a grounded sense of who you are.

Another component of self-management is the health of your physical being. People think that being healthy has no bearing on your emotional intelligence, but it most definitely does. Are you as healthy as you need to be? Are you eating the way you need to be? Are you sleeping the way you need to be? If you want to be emotionally intelligent, you have to take care of your health. Oftentimes people take care of their emotional health but lack on their physical beings. How can you say you're going to be nice to people if you're cranky because you are tired? If you have a tendency to get angry, this can definitely affect your relationship management. Best believe, when you are upset, you will not be able to respond to people in the most constructive way possible. These are simple examples of how your health affects your emotional intelligence, but let's take this example further. What happens if you are overweight and you have chronic illnesses such as diabetes or asthma? You will definitely find yourself with challenges that people who are healthy will not have to run into. Not to say that people who are sick cannot be emotionally intelligent, because they can. The point I want to drive across is that physical health and physical well-being only makes your emotional intelligence stronger.

You remember the biography or obituary that you wrote earlier? How did you envision your life? Were you taking medication for the rest of your life or were you in pretty good health? Now is the time to act to your commitment to be physically healthy if you did not do that before. Now I know it is not easy if you have to switch gears in order to be physically healthy but it is necessary. Do you need to bring intermittent fasting or another type of diet that fits your lifestyle? Now is the time to do it.

The next key to self-management is overlooked just like your health, but it is nonetheless important. That is how you breathe. Breathing is often times called the life force and not without reason. Breathing is used to reduce anxiety in many people, thus a wonderful de-stressor. If you become a pro at breathing deeply and from your diaphragm, you are able to stay calm no matter what situation you find yourself in. To start practicing deeper breathing, you want to get comfortable and breathe in as deeply as you can for 10 to 15 seconds. You can repeat this exercise 2 or 3 times a day until you become used to deep breathing as second nature.

The next step to continue is to work through your painful memories. This step to becoming better at self- management is likely one that is going to be most painful. It builds on your memories from the previous chapter. This step includes continuing to heal yourself from past traumas. Anything that has happened to you in the past that is bogging you down will prevent you from being the best and most intelligent person you can become. Continue to work through those experiences. To represent your total peace, you can burn your journal once you finish. This is a representative of you moving on from childhood trauma. This will give you a burst of positive energy, a new outlook at your self-esteem, and a power to go forth in your new journey to become emotionally intelligent. If the trauma or memories of your childhood experiences are still very overwhelming for you at this point, you may want to consider seeking out help. Seeking help for an issue is not a sign of weakness — it is a very important aspect of healing. If you have insurance, you can check with your insurance provider to see if it will cover your therapy. Even if you do not have insurance, sometimes your workplace has a special hotline you can call if you contact your employer's human resources department. If you have limited resources and no insurance, you can then try to find a nonprofit to see if they offer any special form of therapy.

If you are caught up in the fact that you do not want people to know that you are going to therapy and it prevents you from seeking out help, you can look for a more private therapist. You can try online therapy which is a popular thing to do nowadays. There are even therapy apps. With a simple app, you have direct access to a therapist and you can talk to them without having anyone to see your face or know that you're going through therapy. The work that you can do with a therapist may prove more fruitful than the work that you do on your own. Yes, you can improve your mental intelligence without a therapist, but sometimes speaking to someone else that has no relation to you or understanding of your personal history can be very helpful when trying to work through your past.

In situations where you are faced with managing a difficult situation, you can try these few tips that will help you buy more time so you can cool down before having to make a difficult decision.

- There first is the trusty step of counting to 10 before you respond. Breathe deeply when you do. You can always take more than one to make sure that you feel calm before proceeding.
- The next step is to create a quick list. On one side, write your emotions and then reasons. Try to figure out why you feel a certain way. Scratch off what may be causing the issue and what may not be happening. Scratch off any reasons that aren't helping. And then what is left, you can see what you can do to improve the situation.

Valerie is exhausted from all the work that she has to do in order to manage her emotions. She feels more confined, but she has noticed that she feels better when people do not run away in fear from her or grimace when she is around. Valerie knows that she has a lot more work to do, but she feels very confident in the work that she has done so far. She will continue to work on managing her emotions and has even considered setting aside a time every day to continue to work on her self-management skills by breaking the tasks into small, manageable baby steps.

Once you get through the task of managing your emotions, the next step is to work on your social awareness.

Chapter Highlights

- Self-management is composed of four different components — physical health, emotional healing, positive initiatives and outlook on life, and relaxation and breathing exercises.
- There are a few exercises you can do to improve your self-management skills. You can make a copy of your obituary and make a commitment to be healthy. You can work on your self-talk skills, create affirmations, and perform visualization techniques.
- You can also get in the habit of practicing your breathing to help you improve yourself management skills when faced with difficult situations.

Do the Work

- Stress-management is also an important part of self-management. What ways have you come up with to handle your stress? Are you going to walk away when you are stressed? Visit your favorite spa, listen to your favorite song, or have your favorite meal? Will you exercise to take your mind off the stressful situation? Come up with three things to do when you are feeling stressed to help alleviate the stress you are feeling.

Emotional Intelligence

Here are some helpful scenarios that can help you with your self-management. This helps you to think through ways to manage your emotions and apply the concepts learned in this chapter. There is no right or wrong answer. You can take this practice to the next level by role-playing with friends.

1. Your co-worker begins to blame you for everything that is going wrong at work. You want to scream and shout that it is not your fault, however, you have been working on your self-management skills. What would be a great way to handle this situation?

   A. You take a deep breath and you calmly explain to the co-worker that it is not your fault. You also constructively advise them how to communicate with you. Playing the blame game is not an effective form of communication for you.
   B. You ask your coworker to refrain from speaking negatively and contact your boss. You let your boss handle it. This situation is above your pay grade.
   C. You fight fire with fire. Being calm has not worked. Being mean is the only way that your co-worker will understand that you mean business. If that doesn't work, you can get physical if they continue to provoke you.
   D. You bring in a third party instead of trying to handle it on your own. A third party will be able to speak to the co-worker in a way that you're unable to.

2. Every time you hear this one song it reminds you of a painful memory. What can you do to try to ease the memory from that song?

   A. Try to see a therapist and see if they can help you. Ask for recommendations from friends or search for a reliable therapist on Google.

Emotional Intelligence

    B. Journal and meditate about the personal experience and find some closure on your own. Also, be open to the fact that some situations do not give you any type of closure.
    C. You can go to the people that hurt you, explain what is going on, and then forgive them. Then forget about the situation. Past is past and let it stay there.
    D. You can try not to avoid the situation and just think about it hoping but nothing can happen by not facing it.

3. Your friend wants advice on something but they are not going to like it. What is the best way to handle the situation?

    A. You can have a talk with your other friends to get them to tell this friend the truth so you do not have to do it.
    B. You can be honest and polite in a respectful tone. Then tell them what you really feel. If they could not handle it, then they should not have asked in the first place.
    C. If your friend is your friend, they will be able to handle your reaction no matter what it is.
    D. It is better to lie and keep the friendship than to tell the truth and lose the friendship. Sometimes the truth is not beneficial at all.

4. There is a person who constantly dismissed your feelings every time you try to explain how you feel. They obviously do not care and continue to do what pisses you off. You can't necessarily end the relationship, but you have to figure out the best way to handle your emotions in this situation. What should you do?

    A. You can give them a big cursing. They do not care anyway. After you do so, hopefully, they will not talk to you ever again.
    B. Avoid them. They are not worth wasting your time on to try and explain to them how you feel.

C. Continue trying and talk to them. Hopefully, they will see the error of their ways and be nicer to you. If not, do not change who you are because of how they are acting towards you.
D. Still be nice to them and continue to express how you feel. By treating them the way you want to be treated, you hope that you can continue to kill them with kindness.

5. You have noticed that the affirmations you have been using are not working as efficiently as they were before. However, you've noticed that you have reached a block. You do not seem to be improving as much as before, but you do not see any drastic things in your life that suggest you are progressing backward. What should you do?

   A. You should create new affirmations and see how they work.
   B. You should create new affirmations and combine them with the other affirmations you are using.
   C. You should switch up your routine and try to throw in some visualization exercises and see if that helps.
   D. You do not need to change anything. Keep going at it the same way and you will continue to notice an improvement. Sometimes you have to have a breakthrough with what you are currently doing before you move forward.

Chapter 5: Building Social Awareness Skills

Valerie has done lots of good work on her self. She has improved drastically in the first two components of emotional intelligence that require work on yourself. However, she now has to combine this work on herself and figure out how to use it when she is with other people. For Valerie, every social setting that she goes to seems to operate differently. The people wear different clothing, they speak differently and she has to act a certain way in each setting according to the instructions from her husband. She's honestly quite confused. She wants to be the same way at all time but notices that most people shift who they are depending on their setting. Her husband had to explain to her that people are not changing who they are in different settings. They are only changing their behavior and doing what is deemed most appropriate. Valerie is now ready for the next challenge of figuring out how to manage her social setting and develop the awareness that comes along with it.

Like Valerie, once you are able to be self-aware and have self-management skills, it is time to layer in building on your social awareness. Social awareness can be difficult because people are complex. They are great at hiding their emotions by lying or not knowing what they want themselves. Because they are not self-aware, they have so much baggage that they are dealing with and project that baggage onto you. However, in order to be a fully rounded emotionally intelligent person, you must know how to interact with people as well.

There's a basic need for humans to feel connected to people. Other basic needs of human beings are to love, to feel loved, and to be valued and affirmed. That is necessary and it is an important part of being socially aware. We are socially aware you are also able to be empathetic and to put yourself in someone else's shoes. Emotionally intelligent people understand that sometimes you have your days and sometimes you have bad days. The flexibility to be able to go back and forth between these understanding is most important. The first part of being a socially aware person is to realize that there is good in every human. There is a tendency to only focus on the negative in people. However, when you know that there is inherently good in people, your reactions and interactions with them are going to be much more positive.

The next component of social awareness you need to develop is knowing how to give the right social signals and how to pick up on other people's social signals. You want to be approachable and friendly. The way to do that is to use certain non-verbal clues. You want to make eye contact with people and do not be afraid to touch them. However, you also have to be aware of how people are responding to your non-verbal clues. When you touch them, make sure that they do not flinch or give you any other key that they do not like it. If you decide to touch people, a simple shoulder touch or hand touch should suffice. You want to be mindful of people's personal boundaries and respect their preferences. Not everyone likes to be touched and that's okay. Another nonverbal clue to be mindful of is your face. Some people say they have a resting angry face. When you are in a social setting and you wonder why people are not approaching, think about your face and make sure you're not scaring people off by your unintentional facial expressions.

Additionally, how you stand is another important factor of being socially aware. If you are always hunched over, it doesn't demonstrate much confidence and people will not be attracted to you. The next thing you want to be able to pick up on your social awareness is if someone is being honest or being disingenuous. It is important to rely on your guts in social settings too. If you meet someone and do not feel comfortable around them, do not ignore that feeling. Do not feel like you have to try to make friends with someone if they do not feel that way. You can also observe people by what they tell you and their actions to see if they have integrity or not or if they are playing games.

The next component of being socially aware is to notice the social environment dynamics and fit in accordingly. This is called an organizational setting and the awareness is described as organizational awareness. In any organizational setting, you have to pick up on certain clues.

- Who is in charge? Who is everyone in the room referring to? Do you see any pictures around that give the level of hierarchy so you can quickly identify the head honcho?
- Who is not in charge? Who are the people in the room being completely ignored or being talked about behind their back? Is the person aware that no one likes them?
- What are the politics at play? Is it the person who is in charge or are they following the instructions of a larger force at hand? Is the person in charge there by nepotism or by their own merit?
- What is the emotional feel of the room and power relationships? Can you see that people are happy to be working with everyone? Does the room feel like its buzzing? Or does it feel depressed or all gloom and doom?
- Are most people generally excited to be there? Do the people look like they are joyful or are they dragging their feet, scowling and looking at you through squinted eyes?
- Are there smaller cliques within the larger organization? Do you notice certain groups of people always gathering around no matter what's going on?
- Are people dressed a certain way?
- What type of language are they using?

- Is the environment relaxed or formal? When people greet you, do they act like they are concerned who you are or do they look right through you?

Again, if you do not have a good feel for this, you can also ask someone that you trust.

Lastly, emotionally intelligent people have a heart to serve. This means that they put others first and are willing to be a servant or help others out. This does not mean that you are a pushover, but it does make people want to work with you. Others will be instantly drawn to you. From there you are able to learn how to be of service and keep solid relationships. So what does socially aware in this look like in life?

To apply and continue to develop these social awareness skills, here are a few skills that can help:

- Truly listen to what people have to say. You can repeat what they say in their own words. Notice how people react to what you're saying and how you're saying it.
- Observe people. People-watching is one of the quickest ways to blend in and quickly pick up on what's going on. You will be surprised by how much you can learn just by being silent.
- Watch your tone when speaking. Try to have a neutral, calm tone while speaking. Talk slowly, yet clearly. If you are soft-spoken, work on speaking in a voice that people can hear you so you do not come off as having low self-esteem.
- Have open-ended questions that you can ask people whenever necessary so you always have something to talk about if needed. You can Google brainteaser questions and pick out a few ready to use in emergency situations.

Emotional Intelligence

- Make eye contact with people. Look at them directly in the eye. Smile. If they look ways, try to turn back the intensity but still do not shy away from making eye contact.
- Say hello to people with their name. If you have trouble remembering names, try to give yourself clues of their names by making associations or alliterations with their body parts.
- Be empathetic. You do not have to agree with what people say or understand why they said it, just be nice about it. In other words, always be willing to walk in another person's shoes.
- Accept positive and negative feedback just the same. Say thank you and try not to defend yourself. Even negative feedback is important. The feedback may not be true, but what they are saying is beneficial because it causes you to have a better understanding of how people perceive you.
- Take ownership of your behavior. Always be willing to be the bigger person. This takes maturity and can be quite difficult initially, but it will definitely help you to move quickly through life.
- Avoid putting yourself in situations that you do not like so you are not uncomfortable. As you get older, you realize that you do not have to do things that make you uncomfortable. Yes, you want to try new things to get out of your comfort zone. However, after being in social settings multiple times, if the vibe hasn't changed, don't feel the need to put you through future torture.

Know your strengths and weaknesses and lean on them when interacting with people so they can see the best in you. Another great way to improve your social awareness is to just have different experiences around different types of people. You can volunteer, travel, or visit a different part of town to observe more people. Just like building all the other components of your emotional intelligence, this is not going to happen overnight. Pace yourself.

Emotional Intelligence

Valerie feels like she is catching on how to change her behavior in different social settings while being true to herself. She has paid careful attention to the dress code and behaviors of different people in settings that she finds herself in. She is now ready to learn how to manage different relationships in her life and this will be the top of the next chapter – relationship management.

<u>Chapter Highlights</u>

- Social awareness is how you react to people and maneuver in a social setting. It builds on the skills of self-awareness and self-management.
- Organizational awareness is all about how you can pick out the dynamics of individuals and groups in an organizational setting. The quicker and most effective way you can do this will help you assimilate in different settings easily.
- Developing empathy and listening skills combined with having a service mindset are all great building blocks to improving your social awareness.

<u>Do the Work</u>

Here are some great scenarios for you to check out and role play. This helps you to think through ways to develop your social awareness skills and apply the concepts learned in this chapter. There is no right or wrong answer.

1. There is a person in the office who is picked on by your boss. You think other people are also bullying this person and it makes you uncomfortable, but you do not want to put your job in jeopardy. What should you do?

Emotional Intelligence

    A. You should ignore them and jump in on the bullying so you will not put your job at risk. This is what knowing the company culture and having social awareness is all about.
    B. You should tell the person to be encouraged and know that you have their back in secret. But in front of everyone else, continue to make fun of them.
    C. You need to report everyone to HR anonymously because your colleagues are not acting in a professional way.
    D. You should speak to the person in charge of your manager to let them know that what is going on. No one likes to feel left out. One only wants to come to work and not feel picked on.

2. There's someone who has told other people that they do not like you, but every time you see them, they are nice to you what should you do?

    A. You should go to the source and ask them if they like you or not. Do not shy away from the conflict. You may find out that they do not like you for reasons you had no idea about.
    B. You should tell them what you heard and get to the bottom of it one-on-one. It's easier for people to be vulnerable and feel less pressure when you are in a one-on-one setting.
    C. You should just ignore them and focus on your work in a group setting. If they have a problem with you, it's their issue, not yours. However, if they continue to push you, say something so they know that you are not a pushover.
    D. Do nothing. Their behavior does not affect your paycheck.

3. You really want to be nice to someone, but you do not want to come off socially awkward. What is the best way to meet new friends?

Emotional Intelligence

  A. You should hang around with people in the lunchroom and quietly listen and laugh. Then try to befriend people one-on-one.
  B. Let people know you are looking for friends and that anyone's interested should contact you.
  C. You should find someone who you think is nice by observing them and ask them if they would like to be your friend in a one-on-one setting.
  D. You should look for the nicest person you can find even though they may not be compatible with you, and ask them.

4. You notice that everyone is honking their horn at someone as they pass the street. You have no idea what they are doing. What should you do?

  A. You should honk your horn too. Other people are doing it.
  B. You should not honk your horn. You have no idea why the people are honking the horn and you do not want to do the wrong thing.
  C. You can ask someone on the side of the road why they are honking at this person. Maybe they can tell you.
  D. You should just keep driving and wave at the person instead of honking. That seems nicer to you.

5. You go to an event and notice that you are severely underdressed. You feel slightly uncomfortable. How should you handle the situation?

  A. You should act normal. There is nothing wrong with not knowing the dress code. Your self-esteem should be so high that even if you were in a potato sack, you would feel comfortable.
  B. You should make a mental note so you will not be underdressed the next time. Also, try to figure out why you had

the wrong perception. Maybe you are not picking up on something in the social setting that is causing you to pick up on misinformation.

C. You should just go home. There is no need to feel uncomfortable. Besides, you can't keep ignoring people pointing and making fun of you all night.

D. You should stay and explain to people why you are underdressed. Hopefully, they will not make fun of you.

Chapter 6: Building Relationship Management Skills

At this point, Valerie has learned how to be self-aware, manage her emotions, and identify the social settings that she finds herself in. However, at this point, she has more obstacles to climb. That is to figure out how to manage the relationships in her life. There is the relationship with her spouse, children, and extended family that she must manage, then there is the relationship with her bosses and co-workers that she must manage as well. Just when she thought that she had enough to figure out, she has to figure out how to manage relationships with her friends too. She knew that there was some work to do. Since being self-aware taught her to know to be in touch with her feelings, she knew that she would have to think about the varying relationship in some type of capacity before she was to move forward and she was absolutely right. Relationship management builds on all three components of emotional intelligence and it is the last layer to master in order to be emotionally intelligent. Relationship management starts with being self-aware of your emotions and actions and then practicing self-management. Relationship management develops your social awareness muscle so you are able to manage the relationships in your life.

Relationships vary. They can be relationships with yourself or with others including family, professionally or romantically. Despite the varying nature of relationships in our lives, one of the most important steps in relationship management is to trust in people. Just like in the social awareness chapter, by seeing the good in people, you will be nicer in your interactions with them, even if the relationship was to ever hit a rocky patch. This chapter dives into how to manage various relationships in your life. Relationship management is a three-step process of identifying the nature of the relationship, analyzing the relationship, and then managing the relationship.

Identifying and Analyzing a Relationship

The first step you want to do in managing your relationships is to identify and then analyze the relationship. To start doing this, grab a piece of paper and then make two columns. On the left column, write down the important relationships in your life. In the right column, you will want to add your analysis of the relationship that answers these questions.

- What do you expect from the relationship? – Some relationships are surface level and others are more intimate. It is important to know what your expectations of the relationship are when you are analyzing the relationship so you will know how to manage the relationship. A word of caution. Not all people see the relationship the same way as you, so in order to make some relationships work, you can adjust your expectations based on what the other person expects from the relationship as well. Whatever they think about the relationship, you have to be willing to accept their perception.

- What you are contributing to the relationship? – Take an honest look and write what you are contributing to the relationship that is helping the relationship meet or fail your expectations for it. Are you doing your part? Or are you placing the blame entirely on the other party of the relationship? Use action-based words and be truthful.

- What is the other party or parties in the relationship contributing? – Relationships go two ways. Based on your expectations of the relationship, what is the other party contributing? Look at their actions and list them. Try to be objective, fair, and give them the benefit of the doubt. Are any of their behaviors in response to something that you did?

- Is the relationship meeting your standards or is it falling short of your standards? – Now is the moment of truth. Based on all the information that you have written thus far, would you say this relationship is successful? Is it meeting your expectations or not?

- Does the relationship make you happy or not? – Sometimes your relationship can meet an expectation but you are still not happy. This metric suggests that you look at the relationship and determine if you are happy or not. If you are happy, great. If you are not happy, is it because of your expectations, something you are doing, or something that the other party is doing? Be honest with yourself. You may be surprised. Whatever the answer is, embrace it. If you find an answer you are not expecting, do not try to deny it. Accept and then plan your next moves accordingly.

- What can you do to improve the relationship? – At this time, you may realize that there is lots of room for improvement in this relationship or the relationship is not salvageable. This metric is important because it focuses on what you can do to improve a relationship. If the other party does not want to improve, you may still have to end the relationship. By focusing on what you can do, you take out the variables that you cannot control.

- Is the relationship worth keeping or not? – You've done a lot of great analyzing, but here is the most important question. Should you keep moving forward with this relationship or not? Some relationships will be unable to get rid of either for familial or professional reasons. In that case, you have to figure out the best way to handle the relationship moving forward. Other relationships you have the option of letting go. If a relationship requires you to put much more time and energy into it that it is returning to your life, you have the option to end the relationship. If the relationship is only one-sided and most of the work falls on you, you may want to consider ending the relationship. However, if you deem a relationship is worth saving or keeping, do all that YOU can do to make the relationship thrive. That way you know that you have done all that you could no matter what the outcome is.

After doing this vital work, the next step is communicating with the other parties in the relationship. If a relationship is one that you want to keep in your life, you have to communicate your thoughts about the relations with the other party to see if they are willing to put the work into the relationship or not. This conversation may highlight that the other person does not value the relationship as much as you do or you may realize that you are on the same page and you both can move forward together. Depending on the relationship, you may not have to check in at all, since the relationship is never going away and the person has no desire to improve this relationship. In this case, you can just do what you can do to manage the relationship.

Even in relationships that are thriving, it is good to check in with the other parties every now and then. Checking in every now and then helps the relationship to stay alive. This allows any grievances to be aired out to make sure that the relationship is solid and everyone is happy. Now that you have determined what you think about relationships in your life, you have to transition towards managing the relationship.

How to Practice Relationship Management

Two important skills are necessary in order to practice relationship management. The first is communication and the next skill is conflict resolution. If you can master these two skills, then managing relationships will be a breeze.

To begin communicating properly, you have to quickly develop how to read what personality type someone is and how to communicate effectively with them. There are four different communication styles. They are the boss, the sensitive, the socializer, and the analyzer communication styles.

- The Boss Communication Style – The boss communication style loves to think big picture and leave the details to the little people. They are focused on actions and results. Being sensitive and patient can be a challenge for them, but they can be sensitive if they work on it. However, they can also be loud, demanding, and disrespectful.

  Types of communicative phrases you may hear them say are: "It is my way or the highway."; "I'm right and you're wrong."; "You do not know what you are talking about. Listen to me." Their body language includes clenched fists, narrow eyes, and hard stares. They may also point their fingers. People can think of them as overbearing and mean. They can also think of them as leaders.

    o How to Best Communicate

      a. Expect them to be direct and blunt. Do not take it personally. This is just how they communicate to get their point across.

      b. Get to the point quickly and do not get off topic. If you take the conversation off course to other topics, they may get angry. Try to get the meeting over as quickly and efficiently as possible.

c. Before you talk with them, think about questions they may ask in advance so you will be prepared to answer their questions with confidence. If you waver, you may lose their respect or interest.

d. Be firm in what you have to say and do not let them bully you. If they see you are weak, they may overlook everything you have to say and it may be difficult to gain their respect or confidence.

o What to Avoid When Communicating

a. Do not try to engage in small talk. They do not care. They may even ask you why you are asking them. Keep your tone professional and to the point.

b. Do not make promises you cannot deliver on. This will drive them bonkers. Always underpromise and overdeliver.

- The Sensitive Communication Style – This communication style tends to defer to others a lot. They seem open and polite on the outside, but their body language reveals otherwise. They may stir up trouble in the background if they do not agree with what you are saying even though they are saying they agree with you on the outside.

Types of phrases you may hear include: "Whatever you would like to do."; "Can't we all just get along?"; "I think it is a good idea but if someone doesn't agree do not be surprised." Their body language may include downcast eyes, hunched, and they nod their head a lot. Other people tend to overlook them and disrespect them and the sensitive communication type may struggle with low self-esteem. However, observe and make sure that they are not being manipulative behind the scenes by sharing misinformation or gossip, crying or forming a clique to get what they really want done.

- How to Best Communicate

    a. Be prepared to answer questions about details with them. Practice being open and acknowledge what they've said throughout the conversation. This will build the trust and confidence that they have in you and they may open up more to you.

    b. Be relaxed with them. Ask them what they think about things. They may not tell the truth so watch their body language. Be enthusiastic about what they have to say.

    c. Have clear deadlines and objectives with them so they will understand what is going on. Always ask for their input. This will help them feel relaxed and at ease.

- What to Avoid When Communicating

    a. Do not try to rush them into making a decision. They may feel pressured and will not say what they really think.

    b. Be open to the idea that they may not like what you are saying. They may agree outwardly, but not really. They may not always voice their opinion out loud. If you hear from others that they are talking about you on their back, do not take it personally.

    c. Try to avoid conflict. They will not respond well. If you do have to offer negative feedback, try to make it as gentle as possible.

- The Socializer Communication Style – This communication style loves to be around people. They are extroverted and like to be the life of the party. Expect them to say things like, "I'm open to getting this done in the best way possible."; "I respect your ideas."; "Let me tell you what happened at this awesome party last night." They also practice non-verbal clues like moving their hands a lot, making eye contact, and lots of laughing and smiling. Others can view them as over-the-top or shirkers.

    o How to Best Communicate

    a. Let your personality and sense of humor show. Ask about their personal lives. However, try not to get off topic. Hedge the questions by putting a time limit on the question. For instance, you can say, "Let's catch up for about 10 minutes before we dive into the meeting."

    b. Be open and engaged when you listen to them. If they get off topic, politely try to steer the conversation back to the topic. You can laugh at their jokes and listen to their stories.

    c. Listen to their ideas but be mindful that they can be overly optimistic and not always realistic. When you offer feedback, ask them to walk you through their thoughts process so you can understand better, but do not ask the question in a sarcastic way.

    d. Take notes so they can look at the notes later. Pictures are also good to use when speaking with them. This helps them to pick up on information quickly since you may have wasted a lot of time entertaining them.

    o What to Avoid When Communicating

Emotional Intelligence

  a. Do not be short or rude. This will look like you do not care about what they have to say and then they may shut down. If they don't trust you, they may not be willing to communicate with you.

  b. Do not try to cut them off. Let them talk and smile along. Then bring up the topic at hand. Be gentle and strategic in the ways you bring them back to focus.

- The Analyzer Communication Style – This type of communicator likes to go into details around how everything works. They are meticulous about the details. They look at you in the eyes and say what they need to say without much embellishment. They are also neutral with their body language and appear comfortable and at ease. If they do not understand something, pay attention and see if they burrow their eyebrows or squints their eyes. Others see them as thinkers and sometimes people may get annoyed with them because of their focus on details.

  o How to Best Communicate

  a. Be organized and be on time. They will do their part to be prepared to the best of their abilities and expect you to be prepared too.

  b. Provide as many pertinent details up front and give them room to work independently. Charts and graphs are good. The more proof you can provide in the beginning, the easier the conversation will flow.

  c. Be open to them double-checking your work. Do not take it personally, rather, value their attention to detail because it is a good character trait to have.

  o What to Avoid When Communicating

a. Do not use negative language when offering feedback. Try to be as positive as possible. Also, do not make personal attacks when providing feedback. Keep the feedback to the details only.

b. Try to keep the conversation on track. Do not ask questions about how they feel. Frame your questions to ask them what they think about the facts.

c. They may not be as open to hearing about your personal life or small talk. So try to keep the anecdotes to yourself. However, the anecdote may just be what is needed to get them to open up. Keep the anecdote about children or pets and then see if they open up or not. If they do not open up, do not push it.

d. Do not belittle them or talk condescendingly to them. Let them know that you value their work or insight and they will go above and beyond for you.

As you think about different communication styles, what is your style? What is your dominant communication style? What is your secondary communication style? Knowing what communication style you are helps you to understand the communications styles better and also helps you figure out how to explain to people the best way to communicate with you.

Most people have a combination of all communication styles so it is ideal to try and pick out the main communication type someone has and then apply the communication style strategies that are closely related to their most-dominant communication style. The more you practice communicating with the various styles, you will be able to be more nuanced in the way you communicate with people.

Another major component of having successful relationship management is conflict resolution. When dealing with relationships, conflict is bound to happen. Firstly, accept that conflict will happen. Conflict is nothing to be afraid of nor is conflict good or bad. Conflict is conflict. It is a human emotion that you will run into at some point in your life so it is good to know that it is going to happen and prepare yourself for when it happens. However, to successfully manage them you need to follow a few steps.

- Wait. When conflict first happens, you can pause for a moment. If you need to take a deep breath and count to ten, do so because it could save you from saying something that you regret. When you wait for a brief moment, it gives you time to collect your thoughts. Sometimes to resolve conflict, you can wait and agree to come back to the discussion once everyone has cooler heads.

- When it is time to resolve a conflict, first try to understand the reasoning behind the conflict. Great questions to ask include:

    o How can the conflict be resolved? - What would everyone deem as an acceptable response to solving the conflict? What are the tangibles and intangibles that can cause the issues to be resolved? Are you angry at a specific action or multiple actions? Knowing this can help you get to the root of the conflict.

    o What do you want out of conflict? - Knowing what you want to get out of the conflict resolution is important because it let you advocate for yourself and for your interest. What are non-negotiable for you when trying to resolve conflict? Also, what are you willing to compromise on? If you know this, this can help save time when in the middle of conflict resolution.

- What triggered the anger? – What event caused the issue to boil over in the first place? Was it one event or a series of events? When you are discussing the conflict, are you discussing issues that occurred after the initial trigger of conflict or are you discussing what caused the conflict in the first place?

- What interests do we both have that will see this resolved satisfactorily? – What are the common issues that both parties have interests in that can cause resolution? Are there things that you both can compromise on so the issue can be resolved quickly?

- Is your conflict a real issue or is your conflict an issue because you are a drama king or drama queen? – The answer to this question requires serious self-awareness. Sometimes we are being dramatic and our emotions cause us to blow things out of proportion. When trying to resolve conflict, make sure that the issue is not because you are upset. Make sure that it is because there is an actual issue at hand.

• Use neutral language. Try not to use language that uses blame language. Instead of saying words like "You did this" or "You did that", place the emphasis on how you felt as a result of the action. Take your time. Great advice is to use the 'Is it kind, it is true. Is it necessary' by Shirdi Sai Baba. If one of these is not met, do not say it. Only say words that meet all of these criteria.

• Do not offend people. Do not go low or make personal attacks. When people are talking, you can repeat what they are saying and try to use the words, 'I understand that you said...' or "I think I heard you say..." This helps the other party know that you are interested in what they are saying. This also slows down your angry response. That way the other party knows that you are listening.

Emotional Intelligence

- View the problem independently of the person. This is a wonderful piece of advice because it helps you remember that the other party is just a person. The behavior is what you have an issue with, not the person. This will definitely help you not say things that you wish you did not say.

- Maintain respect. Some relationships last a lifetime so you do not want to say something that will hinder the relationship down the road. When you say something, remember that you cannot take it back. Therefore, mind what you say because it could be the source of further conflict down the road.

- Try to understand first and then try to be understood. This helps you to let the other party feel understood, builds trust and lets them know you are trying to resolve the issue.

- Talk from a place of sadness, not anger. When speaking from a place of sadness, it allows you to be more vulnerable than when you are angry. It also opens up your senses to be nicer to someone else since you are in a vulnerable state.

- In the same vein, try to be open to other people's perceptions. Some people may perceive things differently than you and that's ok. Be open to listening to their perception and take responsibility for offending others even if you did something unintentionally.

- Take responsibility quickly if you are at fault. Take responsibility quickly sometimes if you are not at fault. Sometimes taking responsibility for issues that you may have not really helped resolve the issue. This is an act of good faith and helps mend conflicts faster than if no one wants to take responsibility. This also means taking responsibility for your feelings. Instead of saying what the other party did, explain the emotion that you are feeling.

Emotional Intelligence

This put your feelings out in the open, clears your chest, and then opens the door to a faster resolution.

- Here's a handy formula to use when expressing your feelings in the middle of resolving conflict:
  - I feel (explain the emotion. If you can draw from your varied emotional library this is a good time to do so.)
  - When you (describe the behavior that made you feel the emotion objectively)
  - Because (what was the result of the behavior)
  - I would like (make a request of what the person can do to resolve the issue in the future. The other party may be open to doing this behavior and they may not be.)

- Go directly to the source of the conflict when trying to perform conflict management efficiently. Do not go to someone else about an issue you are having with someone else. This creates more layers that may have to be resolved later on down the road. When you feel an issue, go to the person who is the cause of the issue and let them know what the issue is. Then let them know you are serious about resolving the issue. After you reach some type of resolution, let the conflict be over. Avoid gossiping about the resolution to others.

- Listen. Be empathetic. Try not to take notes while listening to the other party. It can give off the vibe that you are not listening to what they have to say.

- Avoid trying to resolve conflicts by using written modes of communication like emails, texts, or letters. This helps because meanings can be lost in translation over the written word. However, if you must write to keep records of the meaning in a business setting, keep the correspondence professional because the written communication could be accessed by superiors in the future.

- Sometimes you can let your final demands that would resolve the conflict go. If you are unwilling to compromise your requests, the conflict may never be resolved. Be willing to compromise. This does not mean you are weak, it means that you have a solution that everyone is ok with and you become the hero.

- If you have to give feedback, frame it with the 'what-what-why' technique for giving feedback. First, explain what happened that causes the issue in the first place. Give examples. Then follow up with what should have happened to make the situation better. You can end the feedback with why this is a better reaction to the said issue and how it will prevent any conflict in the future.

- If you need a break in the middle of resolving a conflict, take it. Then come back to the discussion. You're human and the other person is human. Sometimes as you discuss the source of the conflict, emotions come rolling back and you or the other party gets upset again. Take the break, take a deep breath, and come back prepared to begin resolving the issue all the way over again.

- Practice. Keep practicing. Conflict resolution is not going to be solved overnight. If at the first time you are not perfect, do not panic. You will continue to improve. You will continue to know how to communicate with others with the communication style that's most effective for them to reach resolutions for conflict.

Communication skills, conflict resolution, and conflict management skills are at the heart of relationship management. These skills with be modified according to what type of relationship that you are trying to manage.

How to Manage Different Types of Relationships

How do you handle relationship management with various components of your family? This section gives you the best practices to use when managing the varying nature of relationships in your life.

Family

You can't choose your family but you can manage your relationship with them. Most people tend to want to have a close family unit, especially with their nuclear family. But in order to do so, you have to manage the relationship. Communication is key in helping you develop the relationship you want to with your nuclear or extended family. Families have so many layers so be careful with how you manage relationships because you cannot change your family. However, when dealing with family if the relationship is toxic, you can be open to cutting off the relationships if after talking, your family members do not want to acknowledge the conflict that you have with them. Do not be disappointed if your family does not always act the way you want them to act. They are human after all. However, here are some great tips to help with managing the relationship with your family.

- Communicate regularly. Be consistent in your communication schedule. With spouses and children, a consistent communication schedule helps them to see how important they are in your life and helps create small traditions among you that build the trust and love in the relationship.

- Consider initiating a regular family meeting for members or your nuclear family. This allows all grievances to be aired out and helps to build rapport amongst the family members.

- For your extended family, try to arrange a trip or time that you can get together outside of the holidays, so you are deepening the familial bond.

Friendships

Some friendships are those that you have to speak to the other person consistently in order to keep the friendship alive. Some other friendships are such that you can pick up right where you left off. You know the nature of your relationship and can adjust accordingly. With the advent of technology, it is easier to stay in touch with friends. Just like any relationship, create a regular communication schedule. With friends, pay attention to what they may not be saying. Be interested in their lives and pick up on any body language that may give their true feelings. Other tips include:

- Evaluate your friendships intermittently to make sure that the relationship is still working for both of you.

- Sometimes friendships change and are not the same. Children, spouse, and jobs can get in between friendships. Allow the friendship to develop organically and maintain the relationship according to changes in your lives.

Romantic Relationship

Relationships can fail when people who are in the relationships stop maintaining the relationship. With a romantic relationship, you have to continue to communicate and trust one another over the length of the relationship. Non-verbal clues are very important to observe in a romantic relationship especially the longer the relationship. When you hug and kiss your partner, how do they respond? When you want to talk and spend time together, how do they respond? Direct communication is also helpful. Check in every now and then and make sure everything is on the up and up.

- Keep things spicy. Do not be afraid to try things. Of course, try only what you and your partner are both comfortable with. It doesn't have to be just sexual things. You can change your routine to add some variety to your lives.

- Set aside time for you both. If you have children together, it is important to continue to bond without them so you can maintain your spark together.

- Resolve conflicts quickly. Conflict management is extremely important in relationships because sometimes conflict can bubble, fester, and damage the relationship beyond repair. The quicker you can resolve an issue, the better.

Coworker Relationship

There is a famous saying that states "Do not be friends with your co-workers." Keep the relationship professional. That's an interesting advice because the type of relationship you have with your co-workers depends on the culture of the office. Some workplace environments are really relaxed where co-worker relationships thrive. Other company atmospheres are cutthroat and competitive. Once you pick up on the company culture, you can decide how to move forward.

- Do not be the negative Nancy in the office. People do not like to be around negative people. Make sure that you are bringing positive energy to the workplace and not bogging it down with your drama.

- Be the co-worker others want to work with. If you are the type of co-worker that works and communicates well, others will want to be around you. This is important because if you ever move up in a company, your co-workers' opinions matter.

- Always respect people. You never know when they may be your boss. Do not let a nasty attitude come back to bite you in the butt.

Ultimately, the most important thing about relationship management, no matter what setting, is to always check in with your emotions. Being self-aware helps you have better relationships. Always check to see that you are being the best person that you can be in any relationship. If at any point, you realize that someone does not like you or you no longer want to continue in a relationship in the same capacity as before, it is your right to change your mind and adjust your behavior accordingly. Always be mindful that relationships can change and be okay with that change. As long as you are doing the best you can do in any relationship that is all that is required.

Other Tips for Managing Relationships

If you have the core skills of communication and conflict resolution, you will be able to successfully manage any type of relationship. Other great tips that you want to have when managing relationships include:

- Let other people know you are acknowledging their feelings. If they have strong feelings of anger or happiness, let them know that you understand their feelings, try to have empathy, but do not dismiss or belittle their emotions. A simple acknowledgment is great because it helps to build trust.

- If you ever get into an intense argument, focus on solutions instead of blaming people. It helps move the conversation forward. Anger is pointless. If at any point you get angry, acknowledge the anger then focus on a way to move forward.

- Be supportive. Always be supportive of people in whatever capacity possible. People never forget how you make them feel.

- Focus on yourself. Do not leave your support systems at the expense of maintaining a relationship. This is especially true in familial and romantic relationships. Do not feel the need to put all your needs aside because if at any point the relationship is lost, you will no longer know who you are.

- The most important thing to remember with relationship management is that you can never change the actions of people, but you can change how you react to them. This piece of advice will save you lots of heartbreak.

- Successful relationships take work. You will not always be compatible with people and they may not always be compatible with you. Everyone will not always like you and you may not like everyone else. That is ok. It is a part of life. Treat everyone the way you would like to be treated and the rest tends to work itself out.

In conclusion, emotional intelligence takes work but it is not impossible. For Valerie, she has learned how to develop her emotional intelligence from scratch and has learned quite a few tips along the way. For her, she noticed how much easier her life has become since she began to develop and embrace emotional intelligence. She is more in tune with herself and her feelings. She considers herself healthier in all aspects — emotionally, spiritually, and physically. She is more in tune with the feelings of others and is able to read what they are saying to her with their words and with their non-verbal clues. Her family life is thriving because she communicates how she feels. Valerie is also able to handle conflict easily without holding grudges or being bogged down in negativity. Her co-workers see how great a communicator she is and her bosses are looking forward to promoting her one day. She would not have been this way if she had not been forced to do so, but she is grateful for how emotional intelligence has improved her life exponentially.

Do not be like Valerie! Do not wait for the relationship to fail, for you to lose your health and mind, or for any other catastrophic incident to happen before you see the importance of being emotionally intelligent. You've made it to the end and the next step is in your hands.

Chapter Highlights

- Relationship management is all about how you handle the different relationships in your life. It is the last step in becoming emotionally aware.

- When you see the good as a core foundation of your relationship management skillset, you will always be able to effectively manage relationships.

- Always pay attention to people's non-verbal clues. It often states how they really feel. Practice adjusting your communication styles and conflict relationship skills to improve your relationship management.

Do the Work

Here are some great relationship scenarios for you to try out on your own. This helps you to think through ways to manage relationships and apply the concepts learned in this chapter. There is no right or wrong answer. You can take this practice to the next level by role-playing with friends.

1. Your significant other has been acting distant lately, but every time you ask them what is wrong, they say nothing is the matter. How should you proceed?

    A. You can take them for the word at it and do not push it. They'll tell you what is wrong eventually.

Emotional Intelligence

   B. You can dig deeper because you know that something bad is going on. They are probably cheating on you.

   C. You can beg them to tell you what is wrong with them because you know something is not right.

   D. You can take them at their word.

2. You were just upgraded to a manager position at your job. You have a co-worker who is having a difficult time in their personal life. Their hardships are causing you to pick up their workload and stay late at work. You want to be empathetic to their needs, but you do not want to stay late at work and do work that you are not getting paid to do. How should you react?

   A. You can talk to them to see what you can do to help that does not require you doing their work. Also, make them aware that they need to do their work or take a leave of absence because it is affecting the team negatively.

   B. You can talk to your boss to see if they can talk to them. That way you are not putting your friendship on the line.

   C. You can be nice to your friend and co-worker so you can maintain the personal relationship outside of work. The hardship should not last that much longer.

   D. You can rule with an iron fist. You are the boss and they need to learn how to handle their personal life and their professional life. You do not want other people on your team to think that you are showing favoritism.

3. Your family loves you and always wants to see that you're thriving. You casually mentioned that you received a salary raise with your new promotion. You have one family member, in particular, who

asks you for money, but do not want to give them the money at all. What should you do?

- A. To test them and see if they really need the money or not, ask them why they are asking you for money. Then create a contract for them to sign before you loan them money. Include the date that they will be paying you back and the repercussions if they do not in the contract.

- B. You just ignore their calls, texts, and emails. They'll be all right. You cannot be responsible for people outside of your nuclear family.

- C. You should get them the loan. If they do not pay you back, never give him another one.

- D. Communicate honestly with them. Let them know you feel uncomfortable with giving them a loan but you still love them. Then deny giving them the loan.

4. Your friendship with your very best friend has changed ever since they got married. They do not keep in touch like before and aren't acting like they were before the marriage. How should you handle the new dynamic in your friendship?

- A. You should realize that things have changed in your friendship and give your friend time to adjust. Everything will settle and go back to normal in the friendship soon enough.

- B. You need to call them and communicate how you feel. By doing this, you ensure that the relationship doesn't get out of hand.

- C. Ignore your friend the same way that they are ignoring you. True friends do not treat their friends like this too.

D. You should end the friendship because they have outgrown the relationship and not being the friend that they need to be.

5. You feel a little out of whack and you are not sure who to talk to about all the feelings you have been experiencing. You discuss the changes with a friend in confidence but soon find out that this friend has told everyone your personal business. How should you respond?

   A. You should not do anything. If they are your friend, they are well within their rights to share your personal information with everyone in your friend group. All of your friends have the right to know.

   B. You should confront them directly and let them know that they should never talk to you again. The friendship is over.

   C. You should bring in all your friend and you all can talk about your issues together. But also let the friend know that you did not like their behavior.

   D. Exclude yourself even more from the group. Everyone is going to think that you are weird anyway.

Conclusion

Thank you for making it through to the end of Emotional intelligence 2.0: A Practical Guide for Beginners. Let's hope it was informative and able to provide you with all of the tools you need to achieve your ultimate goals whatever they may be.

In this book, you have learned what emotional intelligence is and the four components that make up emotional intelligence which are self-awareness, self-management, social awareness, and relationship management. Self-awareness is all about being in tune with your emotions and behaviors, while self-management is all about how you manage said emotions. Social awareness is how you can observe and pick up on the dynamics of social settings and relationship management are consists of identifying, analyzing, and managing the varying relationships in your life. Each component works together and can be improved. You can decide to tackle each component one by one so you do not feel overwhelmed when trying to improve your emotional intelligence. The journey to improving your emotional intelligence is a marathon, not a sprint. So there is no need to rush. Instead, commit to making steady baby steps.

The next step is to start to put what you have learned in this book to use. Do not delay. The longer you wait, the greater the wait to mastering emotional intelligence. Do not be surprised to see the amazing results that daily attention to improving your emotional intelligence will bring. You can re-visit any section of this book at any time in order to reference what was taught. Thank you for taking the time to read this book.

THE MINDFUL PATH TO SELF-COMPASSION

Discover How To Positively Embrace Your Negative Emotions with Self Awareness and Self-Acceptance, Even if You're constantly Too Hard On Yourself

Table of Contents

Introduction 96
Chapter 1: Understanding the Self 99

   Discovering the Multiple Selves 100
   Relationship with Ourselves 102
   Everyone Has Their Own Filters and Explanatory Styles 103
   Your Environment and Your Values 106
   Discover and Understand Your Emotions 108
   Explore Your Fears and Insecurities 111

Chapter 2: Self-Compassion 114

   Buddhist Psychology on Self-Compassion 115
   Why Self-Compassion Matters 116
   Benefits of Self Compassion 117
   Misconceptions about Self-Compassion 120
   Balancing the Act of Generosity 123
   How to Develop Your Self-Compassion 125

Chapter 3: Self-Acceptance 128

   The Myth of Perfection 128
   Allowing yourself to be Imperfect 130
   Making Peace with Your Past 132
   Revisiting Bad Memories and Difficult Emotions 134
   Finding the Silver Lining of Your Past 135
   Accepting Your Past and Moving On 136
   Accepting Your Shortcomings 138
   Accepting Your Future Self 141

Chapter 4: Silence and Self-Criticism 144

   Turning Self-Criticism into a Gentle Supporter 144

Activating Your Growth Mindset 147
Dealing With Your Mistakes 153
Moving on after You've Made an Error 154
Letting Go of Overthinking 156

Chapter 5: Mindfulness and Self-Awareness 160

Practicing Presence 161
Feeling Deeply and Moving On Completely 162
The Value of Daily Reminders 163
Meditation for Mindfulness and Self-Reflection 165
Mindfulness Exercises for You to Try 168
Self-Reflection Exercises for You to Try 169
Tracking Your Progress 171

Conclusion 173

Self-Compassion

Congratulations on purchasing Self Compassion: The Mindful Path to Understand your Emotions, and thank you for doing so!

Every effort was made to ensure it is full of as much useful information as possible. Please enjoy!

Self-Compassion

Introduction

Fostering a sense of self-compassion and self-acceptance can be challenging even for a healthy and well-rounded adult. Despite how important these two characteristics are, very few people are taught about how to utilize them in their personal lives. Instead, we are often taught to be hard on ourselves, push ourselves as far as we can, and demand the maximum results out of our efforts. While challenging yourself to achieve substantial growth is valuable, pushing yourself to the point where it becomes self-sabotaging is not a positive habit to support.

If you truly want to achieve all of the success that you desire in life, you need to have a clear understanding of your mental wellbeing and around how you can support it so that you can improve your chances of succeeding. Without a strong mindset to back them up, most people will fail to achieve their desired level of success because despite having the best of intentions, they will struggle to keep themselves focused and motivated. Through the emotional and mental self-sabotaging behaviors such as having an overly harsh inner critic or trying to push through challenging emotions without acknowledging their purpose or healing them, they will simply burn out and fail to thrive.

As you listen through this book, realize that you are going to be granted every single tool you need to begin developing the skills to become more self-compassionate and self-accepting. From identifying how to feel your emotions and develop a relationship to building a productive mindfulness and self-awareness practice, everything is devoted to helping you motivate yourself in a healthy way. The tools in this book will not encourage or motivate you to become complacent, lose focus, or stop aiming for your dreams with any less intensity than you already have been. Instead, they will support you in having a stronger focus on how you can achieve your goals without compromising your inner sense of wellbeing. As a result, all of the success that you earn in your life will feel far more meaningful and positive.

If self-compassion has been particularly challenging for you until now, or if the concept itself seems foreign, I encourage you to really set the intention to approach this book and the subjects within it with an open mind. You will get the most out of each chapter and all of the tools provided if you give yourself permission to see things from a new perspective at least for the duration of this book. Fully embrace the practice of not only learning about and understanding these concepts and tools but actually working towards putting them into practice in your life as well. As you begin to see just how powerful they are and how they support you in moving forward towards a more positive future, you will quickly begin to realize why they matter so much.

Lastly, there is one major concept that you need to realize before you begin listening this book. That is — self-compassion is an act of self-care, but it is also a tool that is learned through personal development practices. You are not going to be able to achieve self-compassion all in one attempt, nor will you truly be able to measure or grade yourself on the level of self-compassion that you currently have or that you develop. While there are ways for you to track your improvements and we will go into detail on those ways later, you need to understand that this practice is solely about helping yourself feel better and feel more positive in your approach to life. By allowing yourself to embody that balance, you will begin to feel far more peaceful overall.

Now, if you are ready to embark on the next chapter of your journey in self-development, it is time that you begin! Remember, self-compassion is a powerful tool for you to equip yourself with, so approach this book as open-mindedly as you possibly can. And of course, enjoy the process!

Chapter 1: Understanding the Self

Your Self or your identity is an important element of who you are. When you consider who you are, the illusion that you come up with is how you identify yourself. Although we tend to believe that our selves are an inherent part of who we are and that our personal beliefs over ourselves are finite and final, the reality is that who we are and who we think we are, typically reflect two entirely different people. Many people fail to realize that there is a difference and often find themselves genuinely believing that they are the person whom they envision in their minds and that there is no other alternative or option. As a result, they may end up developing a highly toxic, unrealistic, and self-sabotaging image or belief around who they are.

Realizing that who you truly are and who you think you are is two different people can come as a sense of relief to many. When you discover that there is a good chance that you do not actually align with the images or beliefs you have created, you realize that there is an opportunity for you to see yourself in a new light. You may even get the opportunity to start seeing yourself more clearly for who you really are, rather than for the illusion that you have been holding onto in your mind. In fact, by detaching from the strict identity you have held onto in your mind, you can give yourself the opportunity to begin experiencing far more compassion towards yourself in your life.

Identity is a rather complex topic that extends far beyond the image we carry of ourselves and the image that other's carry. In fact, there is an entire psychological study devoted to understanding identity and your sense of self and helping you discover exactly "who" you are. This field of study is known as social science and is comprised of psychologists and researchers who are actively seeking to understand identity to an even deeper level and get a clear sense of what makes a person's identity. Because there are so many different levels of identity, the study itself is quite expansive and continues to discover what one's true identity is versus the way they identify themselves and the way others identify them. In the following sections, you are going to get a deeper insight into what your sense of self truly is, how it is made up, and how your sense of self impacts the way you live your life.

Discovering the Multiple Selves

There are two ways that people have multiple sense of self. The first way that you can experience multiple senses of self comes from how you interact with the people around you and the identity you possess around these people. For example, the self you are around your friends is likely quite different from the self you are around your family or your co-workers. Your environment is a huge factor in which role you will play, depending on where you are and who you are actively surrounded by. The second way that you experience multiple social selves is determined between the way you perceive yourself and the way others perceive you. Since everyone has had their own unique interactions and experiences with you, it is not unreasonable to realize that everyone sees you slightly different from how others see you. For example, your best friend may see you completely different from how your other friends may see you, or your Grandma may carry a completely different belief of who you are compared to the rest of the world. The relationship that people share with you, the experiences that you share together, and their perception of you and of people in general will all impact how people identify you. As a result, you actually have multiple identities – and no, that does not mean that you are having an identity crisis or that you have something wrong with you. It is actually entirely normal to have many identities.

When it comes to identifying yourself, you must realize that on a psychological front, you are not identifying yourself as one person inhabiting one body. You are identifying yourself based on the actual identity that you carry or the characteristics and personality traits that you are perceived to have. Your "self" is the conscious aspect of you that interacts with the world around you, communicates with other people, and shares experiences with others. Although there is no scientific evidence that proves that there is an out-of-body "self," most psychologists believe that the self is not attached to or identified by a person's body. Instead, it is the dimension of you that exists in your mind or the aspects of you that make up "who" you are beyond your physical and biological self.

This part of yourself that is not defined by your body or biology is typically described in three related but separable domains when it comes to psychological understanding. This means that there are three elements that coincide to make up your "self" or your identity. The first domain is known as your experiential self which is also known as the 'theatre of consciousness.' This part of yourself is identified as your first-person sense of being or how you personally experience the world around you. This part of yourself remains consistent over periods of time which results in psychologists believing that it is very closely linked to your memory. The second part of your identity is what is known as your private self-consciousness. This is your inner narrator or the voice that verbally narrates what is happening in your life to you privately within your mind. When you are reading, learning, or interpreting the world around you, this voice is actively narrating how you are interpreting that information and what sense you are making of it. This is the part of you that carries your beliefs and values about how the world works. Neuroscientist Antonio Damasio calls your private self-consciousness your autobiographical self because it is regularly narrating your autobiography in your mind. The third and final dimension of your identity is your public self or your persona. This is the image that you attempt to project to others through your actions, attitudes, behaviors, and words. This is the part of your self that other people interact with and see which results in this being the part of yourself that people generate perceptions around. It is through your persona that people determine what your identity is according to them and their own understanding.

With all that being said, the multiple selves that you embody comes from the persona that you share with others. People will then generate perceptions around who you are, what your identity is, and how they feel about that. It is through this persona that people will decide if they can relate to you, if they like you, and anything else relating to how they feel about you. In realizing that people generate their perceptions of you based off of one single aspect of who you truly are, it helps you realize that their perspective is not accurate. In fact, neither is yours. No one, including yourself, *truly* knows who you actually are. Everything is just generated based on beliefs, values, perspectives, and understandings that have been accumulated through varying life experiences.

Relationship with Ourselves

The relationship that you share with yourself often develops somewhere between the first and second dimensions of your identity. The way you interpret and interact with the world around you, combined with your beliefs and values helps you generate a sort of self-awareness that allows you to begin determining what you believe your identity is. Again, just like with other people, your identity is largely based off of your perception and understanding of the world around you and how it works. Even if your own perception is rarely accurate when compared to who you actually are which is a unique blend of all three layers of your dimensional identity.

Self-Compassion

Because your relationship with yourself is largely defined by your beliefs and values and your ability to live in alignment with them or not, it is easy to realize that how you identify yourself can be easily shifted based on your perceptions. If you carry certain core beliefs about how people should live, for example, and you are not living in alignment with those beliefs, then you may generate a perception that identifies you as someone who is bad or unworthy. You might relate yourself to the identities you have mentally designed for other people in society who you believe to be bad too which can result in you seeing yourself in an extremely negative light. If you carry certain core beliefs about how people should live and you *are* living in alignment with them, you may praise yourself and see yourself as good and special. You might then find yourself relating more to people in society who you see as good and positive, thus allowing you to cast yourself in a positive light.

The reality is that none of us are truly inherently good or bad, we are all just perceiving, experiencing, and responding to the world around us. Generating internal images of what is positive and what is not only results in you setting standards for yourself on how you should behave. If these standards are beyond what you can reasonably achieve or do not align with what you genuinely want in life, then you may find yourself adhering to beliefs and values that are actually rather destructive. Instead of helping you live a life of contentment and satisfaction, you may find these beliefs leading to you constantly feeling incapable and under confident. As a result, your relationship with yourself may deteriorate because the way in which you view yourself is not reasonable or compassionate.

Everyone Has Their Own Filters and Explanatory Styles

To help you develop your understanding of how your perception of yourself varies from other's perception of you, let's discuss personal filters and explanatory styles. Understanding why everyone has such different views of the world allows you to have a stronger understanding as to why there are so many aspects of your identity based on your own personas and the way that people perceive them and you. The concept of personal filters and explanatory styles is simple. A personal filter is how you see the world and your explanatory style is how you explain it to yourself and to others.

Every single person has a unique filter and explanatory style that is based on their own unique experiences in life. All of the interactions they have had, the situations they have encountered, and things they have been told by the people around them shape the way that they view life itself. How each of these small yet impactful things come together will shape how each person perceives the world around them, others that cohabit the planet with them, and themselves. So, for example, if someone along the way has learned that not washing your dishes every day is a sign of laziness and ignorance, then that person is going to believe that anyone who leaves dishes in the sink overnight is somehow "bad," including themselves.

The foundation of a person's filters and explanatory styles are rooted in childhood when a child is not yet able to generate their own independent thoughts and beliefs. Until we are six years old, our ability to critically think about things and generate our own opinions independent of the opinions of others is virtually non-existent so we absorb everything we learn. This means that anything your parents said, people around you were saying, or you were shown through other's behaviors and actions were anchored into your mind as the foundation of your personal beliefs and values. Even though you gained the capacity to think critically and start generating your own opinions around six years old, you were still actively internalizing what everyone told you because, in most cases, no one ever taught you otherwise. As a result, you likely have many different beliefs and values that stemmed in your childhood which have gone on to impact you for years to come. In fact, these very beliefs and values are believed to make up a lot of what your autobiographical-self narrates to yourself on a daily basis, thus shaping the way you see yourself. See, who you think you are may not even be an accurate reflection of how *you* think, it may actually be an internalization based on the beliefs and values you were taught by people as you were growing up.

Since every single person will hear different things throughout their lives even if they are raised in similar environments, the way that every person views and interprets the world around them varies. Even siblings will grow up to have different perceptions and beliefs based on the way that they have internalized the beliefs they heard and were shown throughout their lifetimes. It is through this process that each person develops their own personal filters and explanatory styles for how they interpret and explain the world around them. Because of this, we can conclude that any beliefs that you have around who you are and any beliefs that others have around who you are do not actually define who you truly are. Instead, they define the belief systems that you have established throughout your life until this point.

When you realize that your beliefs are what shape your *perception* of your identity and not your identity itself, it becomes a lot easier for you to have compassion for yourself. You begin to realize that how you see yourself is not necessarily a true reflection of who you are, but instead a way that you have been lead to view yourself. This view was designed to support you in feeling connected to your 'tribe' or family and community, but in some cases, it can become destructive and result in you feeling deeply disconnected from yourself. When that happens, realizing that you are not inherently 'bad' or 'wrong' because you do not feel like you fit in makes it a lot easier for you to have compassion for your feelings and for the experiences you are going through. As a result, healing from these painful emotions and moving forward into a more self-compassionate and self-loving future becomes a lot easier for you.

Your Environment and Your Values

We have already discussed the nature of values but you may be wondering where *exactly* your values come from and why you develop them in the first place. In "The Four Agreements" by author Don Miguel Ruiz describes humans as being self-domesticated creatures. His take on it is that we learned how to organize ourselves into societies and develop basic rules and regulations for those societies. These rules are designed to keep us safe and help us all work together to contribute to the greater good of society without the vicious outbursts of quarreling or fighting to the death like we often see happening in other species. In order for us to adhere to these rules and continue working together as a society and not be punished by society for breaking those rules, we develop values. These values help us determine what is right and what is wrong so that we can navigate domesticated living and continue being accepted by and welcomed into our society. When we act 'right', we are appreciated, loved, and nurtured. When we act 'wrong', we are punished, shunned, and outcast by our loved ones or our community.

Rules and values are generally a very positive thing that helps us to maintain a positive society that continues to operate effectively and productively. When it comes to looking at our communities as a whole, these support us in determining how we can all cohabit our cities, provinces or states, countries, and continents in a way that is consistent and agreed upon. Although not every locality is governed in the same way, the way that each locality is governed is agreed upon and is accepted by other governed localities. That way, everyone is able to coexist without having to experience the worry of being harmed by anyone else in the community and if it does happen, the person who committed the harming will be penalized for their actions.

Of course, society has its flaws and not everyone is held accountable for their actions, but the general structure works towards keeping everyone together and keeping our societies 'civilized' and functional. Unfortunately, the structure ends up falling down into cliques or areas of society where the specific values and beliefs are more strict and specific than the general society. In a standard society, the values and rules are generally simple. Typically, they involve things like do not harm others and obey the laws so that everyone cooperates in a uniformed way that minimizes the harms to others and keeps the society functioning and moving forward. In subsections of society such as within different cultures, religions, neighborhoods, or even within families and social circles, different values often arise. Typically, these values are a lot more specific and restrictive than the overall values of any given society. These also tend to be the values that we adopt throughout our lifetimes and are the foundation upon which we decide everything including right from wrong. Through these more restrictive values, we are typically lead to walk a very specific path in order to keep us being accepted and loved by our social circles. We learn these values through our parents' parenting styles, the words of our friends, and the harsh words of bullies. As we listen to the people close to us communicate, gossip, and either praise or reprimand each other for their behaviors, we develop an inner system of values. These values are meant to help us fit in, not only with society as a whole but with our subsection of society within which we were raised. This is how we are able to stay close and connected with the people that we care about and accepted into our personal 'tribes.'

Where our environment can begin to become toxic is when it supports us in developing values that do not actually match our personal beliefs and opinions. For example, say you are raised in a community that believes in Christian and Christian teachings, but you personally feel a deeper connection with Buddhism and Buddhist teachings. In this scenario, the values that you have learned throughout your life may prevent you from pursuing your desired life path because you fear that you will be shunned or punished by your loved ones. Although you would not be reprimanded by society as a whole, you would likely experience friction with the people you are closest with which could make it feel as though you are being completely abandoned or separated from your 'herd' or group. The fear of being separated results in you feeling the same sensations that a wild animal may feel if they were separated from their own herd — anxious, fearful, stressed out and worried about their ability to survive. Of course, choosing to go your own way in a civilized society will likely not result in overly negative or life-threatening repercussions but it is definitely a stressful experience.

The very fear of being shunned leads many people to find themselves accepting and living by values that are not their own so that they can avoid having to be isolated from their group. As they continue to adhere to the values they do not personally believe in, the person will continue to generate feelings of 'I am bad' or 'I am wrong.' These feelings will continue to grow as long as the values a person is accepting and living by are not in alignment with the beliefs that they genuinely have inside. You may understand exactly what this feels like if you are currently living in a state where the values that you are attempting to live by do not accurately reflect how you feel about life itself.

Discover and Understand Your Emotions

Although values can be powerful in helping societies grow together and stay functional, they can also lead to deep inner struggles with varying thoughts and challenging emotions. This is especially true for people living in an environment that does not accurately reflect their personal values and beliefs. The more you live out of alignment with your personal values, the more your autobiographical voice will become plagued with negative thoughts that bully you. The words you have heard from your own bullies or as others were gossiping about people who were not deemed "acceptable" by your group will ring through your mind. Each time you behave or think in a way that you know would be considered bad or wrong by your group, you will play out thoughts in your mind such as 'Why can't I just be normal?' 'Why am I so bad at everything?' or 'Why can I never get it right?' As these thoughts continue playing out, you will find yourself feeling a deteriorating sense of self-esteem and self-confidence. Your ability to feel worthy and capable will diminish as you continually hold yourself up to standards that do not accurately reflect what you value or believe. In order to step out of the traps of these negative values and belief systems, you have to begin exploring the emotions that are keeping you trapped. You need to begin paying attention to how you are feeling, what your different thoughts are bringing up for you, and how your emotions are impacting your life. By assessing your overall emotional state and getting really clear on what you are actually feeling inside, you can begin to discover whether or not you are actively living in alignment with your *true* values. If you are not, you will need to begin making changes so that you can start living a life that feels more aligned for you, which we will get deeper into later on.

In the meantime, recognizing your ongoing emotional state will give you a general idea as to whether or not your current sense of self is accurate and productive or inaccurate and destructive. If you are living in a chronic state of emotional turmoil and consistently feeling overwhelmed, worthless, unmotivated, or plagued by low self-esteem and low self-confidence, you can pretty much guarantee that your perception of your identity is flawed. It is likely that you are presently struggling to meet your personal values so your autobiographical self continues to attempt to help you 'fit in' to an identity that you do not actually fit into. As a result, each time you act out of alignment with that identity, your autobiographical self reprimands you the same way that people in your group or society would reprimand you if they knew what you were doing or thinking. Although the function of this aspect

Self-Compassion

of yourself is designed to help you fit in and stay protected, it can also become highly damaging and create intense feelings of self-loathing and unworthiness. For that reason, it is important that you identify if and when it is acting out of your best interest so that you can take back control and begin acting in deeper alignment with who you *really* are.

If your emotions are generally positive or content but you find yourself occasionally feeling intense bursts of emotional turmoil, chances are you are living in alignment with your core values for the most part. However, there are likely specific times in your life where your personal values and the external values (or the values of those around you) are not in alignment. As a result, you may find yourself feeling angry, sad, or fearful because you worry that if you do not meet the values of the other person, you will not be 'accepted.' In this case, you may not need to make as drastic of changes, but you will still need to take control over your mind, your inner beliefs, and your chosen behaviors to ensure that you are staying true to your inner self.

The best way to discover and understand your emotions is to begin journaling on a regular basis. Writing down your thoughts, feelings, and experiences when you have a particularly intense emotional response to the world around you or reflecting on them at the end of each day gives you the opportunity to identify what you are actually feeling. As you journal, seek to accurately reflect everything that you are truly feeling by getting to the root of those emotions and identifying them by their true name. So, if you are feeling a sense of jealousy towards someone because they seem to fit in better than you do, make sure that you label that emotion as jealousy and not as something like anger or frustration. That way, you can honestly understand what it is that you are feeling and give that emotion the acknowledgment that it craves. You can also then look into identifying *why* you are feeling that emotion by writing down what beliefs or values you have that lead to that emotion coming up in the first place. If you are unsure, simply analyze your thoughts and see what they suggest. For example, if your thoughts were reflecting jealousy because you wanted to fit in and you felt like another person fit in with *ease*, then the belief that you have may be that fitting in with people should be easy. Because you were not experiencing ease in fitting in or you had to work so hard to defy your own personal values, you may then feel like you are bad or there is something wrong with you because it was not easy for you. In reality, it likely is easy for you to fit in, so long as you are hanging out with the right people who accurately reflect your values and beliefs. I recommend writing in this journal at least once per day so that you can begin getting a clearer understanding of your emotions, your values, and how your life may not be reflecting your values. As you begin to see this on paper, having compassion for yourself becomes a lot easier because you begin generating answers as to why you are not presently feeling like a person who is good or worthy.

Explore Your Fears and Insecurities

As you write down your emotions in your journal, chances are you will begin to generate a lot of entries that revolve around feelings of fears and insecurities. Your fears may sound silly or nonsensical in the grand scheme of things but realize that the very fact that you are feeling them makes them valid and worthy of being acknowledged and healed.

The fears and insecurities that you document, particularly if you discover that you are living largely out of alignment with your values will likely sound something like this:

- "I am afraid that I am not worthy of love."
- "No one loves me because _____."
- "If I change _____ I will have no one left."

Self-Compassion

- "I do not deserve to have my own path or way of doing things."
- "If I make a change they will not accept me."
- "I will be bullied if I act my own way."
- "My decision to go my own way could lead to eternal damnation."
- "(Your religious leader/deity) will not accept me if I honor my own values."
- "I am not allowed to be different."
- "I might die completely alone if I make any changes."

Fears and insecurities around losing the things that you have and around being unloved or unworthy of receiving love in your life if you choose to live in alignment with your own values is common. Many people who are living deeply out of alignment with their sense of self continue to live that way because they worry that if they honor their own belief or values then they will lose everything. The idea of losing their loved ones, their rite to heaven or a positive afterlife (if you are religious,) their status, their home, their worthiness, or any other thing they value is enough to keep them trapped in values that do not actually serve them.

Often, these fears are developed in childhood and are never challenged or adjusted as a person grows up. Although these fears are rarely an accurate reflection of what would happen if you were to begin living in alignment with your own values, the fear still exists. Until you choose to challenge those fears and really get to the root of them and heal them, you will continue living in a state of fear and discomfort even if those fears are unfounded.

The best way to challenge your fears is to ask yourself one very simple question: "and then what?" In asking yourself this question, you allow yourself to continue playing out the scenario of what might happen if you follow your own values until you reach the point where you realize that it is unlikely that anything bad will happen.

Chapter 2: Self-Compassion

In our modern society, we are taught to apply as much pressure to ourselves as possible to attempt to get further ahead in our success. We often hear of various resources that are available surrounding the topics of "how to grow faster" or "how to achieve your goals sooner." What we rarely hear, however, is how to be compassionate with ourselves when we are not moving at the hyperspeed that society tends to dupe us into believing that we are meant to achieve. As a result, very few people truly know how to experience self-compassion when they are in a rut, struggling to advance in life, or not moving at the rapid pace that society deems as being "acceptable."

When you are unable to be compassionate with yourself, you end up putting even more pressure on yourself to achieve things that are simply not achievable within your realm of existence at that moment. Instead of being compassionate with yourself, you find yourself applying even more pressure to try and "jump start" the next level of your success or your life when, in reality, all you are doing is making yourself feel even worse. Rather than feeling motivated and ready to get into action, you end up feeling a lack of motivation and a deep inner feeling of not being good enough or worthy enough to achieve the success that you desire. In reality, your inability to move forward has nothing to do with you not being good enough or worthy enough, but everything to do with you not being compassionate enough. What you really need to be doing is showing yourself compassion, taking the time to understand why you are struggling, and equipping yourself with the tools that you need to overcome your emotions and take the next steps in your life. Sometimes, the fastest way through a hard time is to slow down and simply be compassionate with your self.

Self-Compassion

Buddhist Psychology on Self-Compassion

In Buddhism, there is a big emphasis on the importance of self-compassion and how it helps literally shift a person's mind. Buddhists often teach self-compassion through the art of meditation which is used to help people not only become more cognitively aware but also more emotionally aware of themselves. Through sitting in mindful meditation, Buddhists are able to begin bringing their emotions to the forefront of their lives and recognizing them for what they are. They may also be able to identify why that emotion exists and what message it has to offer the person engaging in the meditation. Through their Zen traditions, Buddhist teachers will educate people on the importance of self-acceptance and self-compassion. In their eyes, these two practices are essential in leading to the state of *shunyata* or emptiness.

In psychotherapy, many positive psychologists have begun researching the concepts of self-acceptance and self-compassion as well. Through studying actions like meditation and self-compassion, psychologists have discovered that one of the easiest ways to predict a person's mental wellbeing both in the present and in the future is to analyze their sense of self-acceptance. A person who accepts themselves is more likely to be compassionate towards themselves as well, meaning that they are less likely to strive to achieve standards of success that do not resonate with their true beliefs.

While self-acceptance and self-compassion have always been valued, psychologists are really starting to understand how these two states of mindfulness are really contributing to a person's overall well-being. By learning how to improve your ability to experience self-acceptance and self-compassion such as through Buddhist meditation, you are able to change your thoughts towards ones that are more positive and productive. As a result, you do not find yourself trapped in a chronic state of feeling disappointed in yourself and as though you are failing in life.

Why Self-Compassion Matters

Self-compassion is one of the most effective mental tools that you could possibly equip yourself with. When it comes to allowing yourself the opportunity to truly move forward in life, self-compassion is a key that will change everything. When you lack self-compassion, seeing yourself as a positive, worthy, good enough, and lovable human being can be extremely challenging. A lack of self-compassion can lead to you constantly striving to do more and be more because you struggle to be compassionate towards yourself when you do not reach unreasonably high standards in your life. This lack of self-compassion can lead to an obsession to become perfect which, as you likely know, is never worth pursuing since perfect truly is not an achievable standard for living.

When you inevitably fail to become the perfect person — the perfect friend, the perfect child, the perfect spouse, the perfect parent, the perfect employee, or any other role you play in your life, you end up feeling immense sadness inside. This sadness leads to you wondering what is wrong with you and why you cannot accomplish the perfect standard that you have set up for yourself. Rather than recognizing that perfect is not achievable and seeing your standard for the unreasonable expectation that it is, you end up seeing yourself as being incapable and unworthy. This type of misconception can lead to deep and painful inner feelings that ultimately lead to you not feeling capable or worthy of moving forward in your life due to an all-or-nothing view.

When you equip yourself with self-compassion, you change your point of view so that you can recognize yourself as being a human who is only capable of achieving human things in your life. Rather than attempting to hold yourself to the unattainable standards of perfectionism, you start to hold yourself to more reasonable and realistic standards that allow you to truly make progress in life. If you find yourself making a mistake or struggling with something, rather than immediately thinking that there is something wrong with you, you can instead focus on being compassionate towards yourself for your experience. Through self-compassion, you slow down, recognize your true emotions, and work through them in a loving and gentle way so that you can fully feel them and move on from them. With your challenging emotions or setbacks completely worked through and set aside, you can easily begin moving forward towards your goals again. As a result, even though you may seem like you are progressing slowly, you are actually progressing faster because you are not hitting extreme levels of burnout and overwhelm along the way. You also stop holding yourself back from your all-or-nothing attitude that leaves you feeling unwilling to begin projects for fear of not being able to accomplish them with perfection.

Benefits of Self Compassion

Self-compassion has many positive benefits that can help you achieve a better life overall. When you are compassionate towards yourself, you essentially give yourself the gentle kindness that you crave during those periods of challenge. Think of your inner emotions as a small child. When you have challenging situations that lead to feelings of not being good enough or capable enough, it is likely that your emotions are frazzled, too. Rather than feeling positive and hopeful, you likely feel fearful, angry, sad, and even embarrassed. As a small child when you felt this way, you would crave the attention of an adult who was more experienced with their emotions that would be able to comfort you and tell you that everything was going to be okay. Likewise, as an adult with challenging or festering emotions, you likely still crave that very same experience — to have someone sit with you, console you through your challenges, and let you know that everything is going to be okay. Of course, as adults, it is not exactly reasonable to believe that we are going to have someone in our lives who can offer that for us every single time we hit a challenge so we have to become that person for ourselves.

That is where the benefits of self-compassion come in. When you begin to become the compassionate, gentle, loving, and kind adult that your inner child needs, overcoming challenges in your life becomes a lot easier. Instead of attempting to whip yourself into submission through abusive acts such as bullying yourself or applying even more pressure to yourself, you instead sit with yourself and console yourself. Through that gentle act of compassion, that part of you that feels abandoned, wrong, shameful, or fearful is able to be consoled and healed. You begin to experience greater feelings of happiness and optimism and your spirit becomes more curious and adventurous. As you continue to show more compassion for yourself, your inner wisdom develops and you become more confident in your ability to have a positive impact on those around you. You experience feelings of hope and faith and your ability to make a dream and pursue that dream is improved because you become a self-starter with a purpose. Since you are no longer bullying yourself into a state of being too afraid to move or make a decision, you are able to open up and move forward with a more positive and optimistic vision of the world and how your life can look.

Becoming self-compassionate does not mean that you won't run into challenges or sometimes experience fear or uncertainty, but instead, it means that you will know how to nurture yourself through those experiences. Through this nurturing ability, you will be able to find a path forward that genuinely feels good and allows you to grow and move with ease. You will break through the chains of pessimism and self-criticism that have been holding you back and begin living with a greater sense of intention and intensity, thus allowing you to move through any challenge you may face with certainty.

Misconceptions about Self-Compassion

The modern world sees things like self-compassion as weak, ineffective, and soft. We are often taught that if we slow down and have compassion for ourselves that we must not be capable enough of moving forward through anything we face. Instead of being encouraged to have self-compassion, we are encouraged to fight harder and continue forcing ourselves forward until we truly lack any energy or will to keep fighting. Because of this conditioning, so many people do not see self-compassion as a positive, uplifting act that can truly help you. Instead, they see self-compassion as a negative, weak trait that proves that you are incapable and that something is wrong with you. This could not be further from the truth.

When you are expressing compassion for yourself, you are not showing a sign of weakness or proving that you are incapable of moving through a challenging obstacle. In fact, you are showing that you are equipped with the exact level of emotional intelligence required to move through anything. People who are self-compassionate know that by being compassionate towards themselves through challenging experiences, they can move through them with greater ease and without lasting repercussions. Through fully working through their emotions and having compassion for themselves along the way, self-compassionate people actually have a far more sustainable coping method than anyone else.

Self-compassion is also not a long-term pity party where you sit around and feel sorry for yourself and the troubles that you are experiencing in your life. When you experience self-compassion, you are not tuning out the bad things or wallowing in how troublesome your life truly is. Instead, you are actually tuning into your true emotions, acknowledging them, and processing those emotions in a complete manner. Through this completed process you are able to

Self-Compassion

move on from the feelings that have you feeling incapable or unworthy and let go of them in a more complete manner, meaning that they will not linger and cause further problems in the future. As a result, you are actually using a very productive and solution-focused approach to your emotions, not one that is allowing you to simply sit around and play the victim of your own emotions.

Another common misconception about self-compassion, especially within people who experience perfectionism, is that being self-compassionate will lead to complacency. If you think that by showing yourself compassion you will be giving yourself an excuse or a pass to avoid having to make any progress in your life, you are carrying a false belief around what self-compassion truly is. Self-compassion is not intended to keep you from achieving anything in your life, if you are using it in this way then you are not using self-compassion but instead, you are using excuses. True self-compassion is not about allowing yourself to do nothing and achieve nothing. It is about being honest and realistic about what you can achieve and recognizing that your personal speed through life is plenty fast enough. You are not required to keep up with some heinous belief that you should be moving any faster than what is reasonable with you — you are allowed to move at your own pace and that is certainly enough.

A big fear that people tend to have is that if they become self-compassionate then they are somehow becoming narcissistic. This is completely untrue. Self-compassion and narcissism are entirely separate qualities and through being self-compassionate you are certainly not at risk of becoming narcissistic. True narcissism comes from an inner belief that you need to be better than everyone else around you and that you will do, say, and think anything that is required in order for you to achieve success in your life. A true narcissist is not someone who seeks to improve themselves genuinely, but rather is someone who feels a deep need to be better than everyone else as a result of a psychological disorder that causes them to see the world in a very disillusioned way. If you are self-compassionate, you are not approaching life through delusion, but instead through a highly intentional desire to actually improve yourself and experience a better life. True self-compassion is not the act of trying to be better than everyone else, it is the act of trying to be better than the person you were the day before.

Another thing that self-compassion isn't is selfish. In many scenarios, people who are expressing self-compassion are told by others that they are being selfish and inconsiderate towards those around them. For example, say that you struggle to have a positive experience at family gatherings because you tend to be treated negatively by your family. Choosing not to attend large family gatherings as an act of self-compassion would not be selfish but instead would be a positive form of self-care and self-consideration. Even though your family may attempt to bully you into thinking that you are being selfish, the reality is that you are simply being compassionate towards yourself and your needs by admitting that you do not want to sit through a negative dinner.

Lastly, self-compassion and self-esteem are not the same things. In recent years, a movement that is known as the "self-esteem movement" has risen to the surface and encouraged people to increase their self-esteem. Oddly enough, following the introduction of the self-esteem movement, narcissism increased with what is known as the "narcissism epidemic." Self-esteem is a word that measures or refers to the amount of confidence that one has in their own abilities or their amount of self-respect. On the other hand, self-compassion is the act of having compassion towards one's self. Unrelated to confidence and self-respect, self-compassion is having a sympathetic concern towards the suffering or misfortunes of yourself or others. When you have compassion for yourself, your goal is not to increase your confidence or your self-respect but instead to increase the amount of sympathy you have towards yourself and your personal experiences.

Self-Compassion

Balancing the Act of Generosity

The myth that self-compassion is selfish likely stems from the idea that people who are self-compassionate are not generous or do not give generously to others. Often times, this myth arises either from people who are no benefiting from another person in their life choosing to be self-compassionate. For example, say you have a friend who regularly asks favors of you to the point that you feel like anytime they call you, you know there is a high chance that they are only calling you to ask for a favor. In this instance, if you were to stop saying "yes" all of the time and start saying "no" because no felt like an act of self-compassion, such as if you didn't truly have the energy or the means to fulfill the favor, your friend might get angry. They may begin to feel that you are being selfish or that you are being unfair when, in reality, you are simply exercising self-compassion by not overpromising yourself to other people.

Just because you choose to be self-compassionate does not mean that you are not going to be generous anymore, it simply means that anytime you are being generous it will be an act of self-love, too. You will no longer agree or promise to do things when you truly want to say no because you recognize that it is not in your best interest when you do, so you will practice self-compassion. Because you are no longer agreeing to so many things that make you feel bad, you will not have a constant feeling of being overwhelmed by doing things that you do not want to do. As a result, the generosity that you give will be more genuine and sincere and it will not weigh you down or lead you to feel overwhelmed or under cared for. This means that you will likely be even more generous towards others, except that your giving will be more focused on doing things that also make you feel good or happy. Through this selective generosity, you will have more energy to share

Self-Compassion

and give and both you and the person that you are giving to will feel positive from what you are both receiving.

In order for you to begin balancing the acts of self-compassion and generosity, you need to start identifying where your boundaries are around giving. If you have never considered this before, chances are that you are giving far more than you truly need to be. This over giving has likely lead to you feeling burnt out, used, unappreciated, or completely frustrated at least once in your life but likely many times. When you begin to address where you feel the worst during your acts of generosity, you can start setting boundaries around these acts of giving so that you no longer feel so depleted after giving to others. For example, maybe a family member constantly expects too much of you and it feels overwhelming for you to attempt to fulfill their demands. Instead of finding yourself trapped in that constant state of overwhelm and resentment, you can start setting a boundary around how much you are willing to give to that person. Maybe you will only give when you genuinely feel like you have the energy, resources, and desire to do so and in all other circumstances, you will say no. This boundary, when upheld, will ensure that you are not depleting yourself by attempting to give too much to the said family member. It will take time for you to identify your boundaries and truly uphold them but once you do, upholding your boundaries and expressing self-compassion in the act of generosity will become much easier for you. Through this act of self-compassion, you will find that giving is more heartfelt and sincere and that you do not feel obligated to give every single time someone asks for something from you.

How to Develop Your Self-Compassion

In a society that fails to truly honor the importance of self-compassion and regularly advocates for the exact opposite, you might be wondering — *"how can I become more compassionate towards myself?"* This answer is completely reasonable and justified, especially if compassion is not something that you have been taught or shown very often in your life. Below, I have outlined three steps that you can begin practicing today in order to start showing yourself more compassion throughout your life.

Practicing Forgiveness towards Yourself

If you truly want to experience the fullness of self-compassion, you need to start practicing forgiveness towards yourself. Punishing yourself for your mistakes and holding yourself in contempt for your failures will only result in you feeling even more terrified about the idea of moving forward in your life. You need to begin accepting that you are not perfect and that it is completely natural for you to experience shortcomings. Everyone has flaws and everyone goes through the process of having to accept themselves regardless of what flaws they may have had in their past, may have in their present, or may develop in their future. The reason why people value you and why you should value yourself has nothing to do with whether or not you are flawed but rather who you are as an overall person. If you genuinely lead your life with a sincere heart and a positive intention, chances are, you are a great person and you deserve to have your forgiveness surrounding the mistakes that you have made in your life no matter how big or small.

Fostering a Growth Mindset

To have a growth mindset means to be willing to focus on areas in your life where you can improve. Many people have a mindset of being "stuck in their ways" or "unable to change even if they wanted to." This mindset is not helpful when it comes to learning how to be self-compassionate as it will prevent you from developing your inner wisdom which typically coincides with developing your self-compassion. By approaching life with a sense of curiosity and a willingness to grow, you not only open yourself up to the wisdom that you need to accept yourself but you also open yourself up to the mindset that you need to accept your shortcomings. A growth mindset means that you are focused on growth, not on perfection, so the idea of failing or making a mistake becomes a lot less scary because perfectionism is not your main goal, growth is. In order to begin shifting your mindset away from perfectionism and towards growth, start focusing on quieting the voice of your inner critic. Avoid comparing yourself to others no matter who they are and start looking for people who inspire you to become a better person. Having role models who also foster a growth mindset and who already have self-compassion or who are working towards it make fostering your own growth mindset far more achievable.

Expressing Gratitude

Gratitude is a state of mind that leaves you feeling genuinely grateful for all of the blessings that you have in your life. When you are grateful, your ability to experience joy and abundance in your life is far superior to when you are not. You also teach yourself to start focusing on more positive things in life so that you can take your focus away from places like your flaws or your shortcomings. A great way to begin developing self-compassion specifically is to start expressing

Self-Compassion

gratitude towards yourself on a daily basis. Each day, look in the mirror and express three to five reasons for why you are grateful for yourself. This could be anything from your willingness to continue learning and finding a way to feel better to your ability to cultivate new friendships and find a company anywhere you go. Try and choose new things every day so that you can start accumulating a list of reasons as to why you are such a great person and why you deserve to have your own sense of self-compassion.

Chapter 3: Self-Acceptance

Self-acceptance is the next step in learning how to have self-compassion. When you develop a sense of self-acceptance, you become far more willing to accept yourself as you are. As a person who features self-acceptance, you allow yourself to become more aware of your strengths and weaknesses and to remain realistic about your talents and capabilities. You also generate a deeper sense of self-worth because you begin to realize that you, like everyone else, are inherently worthy and that there is nothing you have to do in order to earn your worthiness. In other words, none of your shortcomings, flaws, mistakes, or inabilities results in you becoming worthless or undeserving. You recognize that you possess a unique set of skills and characteristics that blend together to develop a person who is certainly worthy and deserving of having and experiencing good things in life.

In this chapter, you are going to discover what self-acceptance is, how it can be achieved, and what you need to do in order to begin having self-acceptance towards yourself. A great place to start is to begin right now by accepting yourself as you are, even if that means accepting the fact that you currently struggle to accept certain aspects of yourself or your life. By having an unconditional level of self-acceptance towards yourself, you open yourself up to the opportunity to be okay with who you are. When you are okay with who you are, having compassion towards yourself for who or what you are not or for the experiences that you have becomes far easier.

The Myth of Perfection

In our childhoods, we are taught that we need to adhere to societal standards in order to be accepted, loved, appreciated, or praised by the people around us. We learn this by being celebrated and praised every time we do something great, ignored if we only do something good, or punished if we underperform. As a result, we are driven to start performing as great as we possibly can every single time we set out to accomplish something. What ends up happening is that our standards for the great increase each time as we realize that upon doing everything great so many times over, people stop praising us because they come to expect that level of greatness from us. For some people, not receiving continual praise from others is plenty because they have learned how to praise and celebrate themselves, so they simply continue achieving what feels like a high standard of greatness within themselves. For others, they crave that praise and celebration so deeply that they will continue to attempt to outperform themselves and achieve as close to perfect results as possible in order to receive positive attention. When they do not receive that positive attention, they take it as a sign that they are not doing well enough and that they need to do even better.

The perfectionism illusion is built even further in the age of social media as people post highlight reels of their lives as a way to try and market themselves as having "the good life." Many diffcrent influential marketers on social media have cultivated a presence that makes it appear like they never experience reality, but instead, they always experience a carefully crafted existence of perfection every single day. For those who find themselves continually attempting to outperform themselves as a result of perfectionism, they may find themselves attempting to replicate those highlight reels in their everyday life. As a result, they hold themselves to standards that even their role models do not hold themselves to which leads to a chronic cycle of attempting to achieve the unachievable.

The reality is, perfect is an unachievable quality that is virtually pointless to attempt to achieve. Even attempting to achieve close to perfect every single time is not ideal as it can lead to you trying to expect far too much out of yourself on a consistent basis. This does not mean that you shouldn't set your goals high or challenge yourself to do better, but it does mean that you should avoid trying to set your goals so high that they are truly unachievable. Achieving near-perfect results from time to time is reasonable and should be celebrated, but setting the expectation that you will achieve near-perfect results every time will only leave you feeling as badly as true perfectionism will.

By breaking down the myth that you have to be perfect or near-perfect at everything that you do, you give yourself the opportunity to start doing your best. You may have heard a teacher, parent, or friend's parent say this to you at some point in your childhood, "Just try your best." That is because, at the end of the day, your best truly is what matters the most as your best proves that you are challenging yourself and working as hard as you reasonably can towards doing better every time. Even minimal improvements are still something that you can celebrate in your life. You do not have to be perfect at everything or even anything in order to be accepted as a positive and worthy human. You simply have to try your best.

Allowing yourself to be Imperfect

For someone who struggles with perfectionism, you may find yourself listening the previous section while mentally disagreeing with it or attempting to justify why *your* perfectionism is different. You may attempt to barter with yourself that you are not like other people or that attempting to achieve anything less than perfect is lazy, weak, or pointless. I want you to stop right now and recognize that these very thoughts are not helpful and they will not support you in achieving self-acceptance and self-compassion. The more you attempt to justify why you are the special person that gets to be perfect while everyone else is just human, the longer you are going to hold yourself to unreasonable standards and stay trapped in a constant loop of self-disappointment.

Being imperfect does not mean that you are not going to try your best, achieve great results, or strive for excellence. It simply means that you are not going to criticize yourself to the point of self-sabotage anytime you attempt something in your life and do not achieve perfect results. When you allow yourself to be imperfect, you open yourself up to the capacity to start trying new things because you become willing to embrace the stage of being a beginner who is inexperienced. You trust that not knowing everything is okay because it simply means that you have more to learn and you trust that you have what it takes to learn *in a reasonable amount of time*. Because you have waived the pressure of being an expert on a new subject right off the bat, you give yourself the opportunity to open up to your growth mindset or the mindset of learning. Through this mindset, you equip yourself with the capacity to learn more than ever before, thus taking you directly towards the very same goal that you were so desperately attempting to achieve with perfectionism.

Unfortunately, allowing yourself to be imperfect is not always as simple as making a choice and allowing your life to transform right before your very eyes. Chances are, you are going to experience many moments of setbacks following your decision to become more accepting of who you are. You may find yourself habitually avoiding things in your life because of your fear of not doing them perfectly or you agree to do them only to find yourself fighting to achieve perfection along the way. Having these experiences is completely normal and they actually provide you with an excellent opportunity to begin practicing self-acceptance right away. You can begin by accepting the fact that you are a healing perfectionist and that you are working towards improving your habits so that you can be more self-accepting, but in the meantime, that means embracing where you are at and consciously changing. As you begin to become aware of these moments or setbacks, start by saying "I accept that I have this habit and I am consciously choosing to start changing it right now. I accept that my best is my best and I am willing to be okay with that being the best that I can offer for this." By saying something like this to yourself, you begin to accept where you are at while still aspiring to make changes and consciously choosing to do so. Remember, you cannot be perfect at breaking your perfectionism. It simply does not work like that. It is going to take time, patience, and practice as you begin to reinforce your new habit of being self-accepting no matter what your best looks like.

Making Peace with Your Past

Part of becoming more self-accepting is being willing to make peace with your past and the way that you behaved or the experiences that you had. You learned about the self and identity in Chapter 1 and now is a great time to recall the auditory self and your experiential self. Chances are the way you experience the world around you and what you are telling yourself through your inner narrator are still heavily linked to past experiences that you have had. Your perception around who you are is likely heavily shaped based on a few highlights in your past, whether they are positive or negative which means that you are probably viewing yourself in a heavily outdated and unrealistic manner.

For many people, their perception of themselves revolves largely around some of their worst experiences in the past. For example, if you were mean towards someone in your past and said something unkind out of a fit of anger and afterward you felt intense guilt around that experience, you may perceive yourself as being unkind, reactive, and mean. This could lead to you believing that you are not worthy of having nice things or being surrounded by nice people because you are too mean and therefore you are undeserving. In reality, you have

Self-Compassion

probably been incredibly nice to many people throughout your life but this is the one thing that continues to play through in your mind and delude you to believing that you are not a good person. If you truly want to move forward and experience a greater sense of self-compassion and self-acceptance, you need to be willing to come to peace with these types of experiences in your life.

You need to develop a sense of trust that who you were is not who you are and that the actions you made no matter how positive or negative they may have been, do not define who you are today. In fact, they have likely never defined who you were, to begin with. Coming to terms with who you were and what you did and accepting that these are all a part of your past allows you to begin accepting yourself and the choices you have made throughout your life. When you begin to accept yourself and your choices, it becomes easier for you to decide to be okay with who you are and okay with what you have done and experienced in your life. That feeling of being okay with your past does not have to mean that you are proud of what you did or that you believe that you have to hold yourself up to the same incredibly high standards as you used to. It simply means that you are willing to accept who you were then just as much as you are willing to accept who you are now which allows you to move forward more gracefully.

If accepting your past is particularly challenging for you, you may choose to move through it at a slower and more intentional pace. Allowing yourself to become okay with just a few things at a time, based on what is relevant to your current life, and moving deeper from there as you go along may be more achievable than attempting to become okay with everything at once. In many cases, your unwillingness to accept your past will arise from a result of you still carrying unexpressed emotions around those experiences. By going through them slowly and with greater intention, you can ensure that you are giving yourself plenty of time and self-compassion to completely feel your way through each memory and move forward more completely as well.

Revisiting Bad Memories and Difficult Emotions

As you move through the process of accepting your past, there is a good chance that you are going to come across many bad memories and difficult emotions. When you arrive at these bad memories or these difficult emotions arise, you may feel an instinctive desire to shut down or avoid working through these memories so as to avoid being overcome by difficult emotions. In some cases, the pain may be too much to bear. In these circumstances, self-compassion becomes even more crucial as you need to be willing to show compassion towards yourself for the emotions that you are feeling towards these challenging memories.

Throughout the process of revisiting bad memories, it is imperative that you refrain from putting too much pressure on yourself to feel better or heal. Trust that by feeling your emotions and by having compassion for yourself, healing is happening and simply be willing to sit with yourself throughout the process. Do not put an expiration date on your feelings or put a deadline on when you want to be healed by. Just sit with yourself and be willing to slowly navigate through the healing as it happens. When you stop putting so much pressure on being healed and you start sitting with yourself as you revisit painful memories and emotions, healing happens naturally. It does not need to be pushed, forced, or sped up, it simply needs to be honored and experienced.

If you have been sitting with the pain for a while and you find that it is particularly challenging for you to sit with, you might consider moving through it more slowly. Rather than attempting to heal in one afternoon, simply allow yourself to recognize the pain and sit with it for as long as you need to before moving back into your daily living.

Revisit that same memory and pain as much as you need to in order to heal it and give yourself as much time in between as you need to in order to become okay with the feelings that you have already felt along the way. By balancing the process of healing with the process of living, you ensure that you are able to continue living your day to day life while also healing the painful memories that you feel burdened by. Believe it or not, the more you are open to sitting with those challenging emotions as they come, the sooner you feel your way through them and the easier it is for you to get back to your day. Attempting to hide them, repress them, push through them faster to get them out of the way or otherwise become too controlling over your expression of your emotions will only result in them lasting longer. When you feel them as deeply and intensely as you need to, then they begin to move out faster and you are able to move on sooner.

The one thing you do need to be cautious about when it comes to challenging emotions is the unsafe expression. As you feel through your emotions, seek to do so in a safe and constructive manner. If you struggle with handling your emotions and find yourself becoming reactive or dangerous towards yourself or anyone else, it may be best to seek professional support in navigating these emotions. That way, you can release them without doing harm onto yourself or anyone else along the way.

Finding the Silver Lining of Your Past

As humans, we possess what is known as a "negativity bias" which results in us primarily focusing on the negative. This is our biological way of being able to recall bad experiences so that we could avoid experiencing them again, but it is not always effective particularly when it is unbalanced or not met with positivity. You need to learn how to balance out your mind so that you can focus on your past in a more balanced and realistic manner to avoid feeling as though your life has been one major negative experience.

The best way to begin seeing your past in a more positive light is to start by journaling all of the great things that happened to you. You should start by writing down all of the bad stories you are telling yourself and looking for the silver lining in those bad stories. For example, maybe your parents were not active in your life but you had a grandparent or an aunt or uncle who was. Maybe you got divorced when you were younger and it was particularly painful, but the beginning of the relationship was magical and magnetic. Maybe you got bullied a lot in school, but being bullied lead to you finding your best friend and to this day you two still remain close friends.

By identifying what negative stories you are telling yourself and choosing to see them as having a silver lining, you do not erase the fact that they are painful or those bad things happened. You simply choose to recognize that it wasn't *all* bad and that you did have many positive experiences throughout your life. When you start to create this sort of mental balance between the good things and the bad things that happened in your life, it becomes easier for you to see that there have been many positive elements to your existence. Accepting your past becomes a lot easier because you realize that, although it may contain a lot of pain, it also contains a lot of happiness.

Accepting Your Past and Moving On

After you have chosen to accept your past and you have decided that you are ready to begin moving forward, it is up to you to decide what that is going to look like. Until now, chances are, you have been carrying on with your life as though you are being held captive by your past choices and mistakes. This means that, in choosing to heal and accept those past choices and mistakes, you also need to choose what

Self-Compassion

it is going to look like for you to move forward. In order for you to do so, you need to have positive forward-focused goals that are going to allow you to relieve yourself of the habits you carry from your unhealed self. These goals can be anything from choosing to see more positivity in your life to choosing to complain less when troubling experiences happen. You want to choose your goals based on what feels right for you and what will reflect the most positive change from your healing in a realistic manner.

When you are choosing to accept your past and move on, a great practice for you to do is to choose to wake up every single morning and forgive yourself for everything you have done in your life that has made you upset or ashamed. By forgiving yourself consciously every single day, you remember to stop holding yourself hostage for the mistakes that you have made and the way that these mistakes have impacted you. You also choose to start seeing yourself as a human who is deserving of compassion and second chances, even if you have made countless mistakes in your past.

If forgiving yourself feels challenging, start small and consider using a journal to track your forgiveness. You can easily write down what you are choosing to forgive and how that feels for you to consider forgiveness around the said topic. Be extremely honest with yourself about the feelings you have around the incident you are seeking to forgive and the blockages that have prevented you from forgiving yourself sooner. As you write these things down, the process of bringing them to your awareness and seeing them on paper will help you begin to cultivate a higher level of compassion towards yourself because you will begin to see yourself as a human with feelings. If experiencing compassion towards yourself continues to be challenging, consider how you might feel towards another person if they were to confide in you about all of the things you have just written down. Chances are, if it was coming from someone else, you would feel a lot more compassionate towards them than you may be feeling towards yourself around this very same subject. Use this understanding to begin developing compassion for yourself and to realize that you also deserve compassion for the troubles you have had in your life because you too are human.

It is critical that you realize that the process of getting to forgiveness and moving on is one that requires patience and acceptance in and of itself. Yes, the rewards of your patience and acceptance will be huge, but you will never achieve them if you do not begin practicing them right away, even if you feel as though you are not ready or worthy enough. The longer you hold onto these fallacies, the harder it is going to be for you to move forward because you will never give yourself the compassion and forgiveness that you need in order to do so. In the beginning, forgiveness may just feel like a subtle shift as you move forward in your life, but over time it will become easier and it will integrate more deeply with your begin. Forgiveness is a process and finding the capacity to begin forgiving yourself is equally as important as finding the capacity to forgive fully.

As forgiving yourself becomes easier and the forgiveness begins to sink in, living your life day in and day out becomes simpler because you are no longer living as a victim of your past. Instead, you begin to fully accept and integrate your past and let yourself off of the hook for troubling mistakes you have made along the way. As you do, leading your life from a clearer and more compassionate frame of mind becomes more achievable and thus your entire life improves because you are leading with your best foot forward.

Accepting Your Shortcomings

Every single human is born with their own perceived set of flaws that they must learn to come to terms with and accept as a part of who they are. From bodily imperfections to emotional or cognitive

Self-Compassion

imperfections, every single person has something that they believe in some way makes them abnormal compared to everyone else. Even the people who seem to have it all or who behave in a way that leads you to believe that they have no flaws or difficulties are people who struggle with imperfections or who have put in a lot of time to accept themselves as they are. Not one person exists on this planet who has not had to overcome the feeling of having imperfections that result in them feeling like they are undeserving of love or goodness or like they are not valuable or worthy. Again, living in a world where social media is as largely praised as it is and people share only their highlight reels, comparing yourself to others and magnifying the intensity of your perceived flaws becomes even more dangerous. So many people believe that they are unworthy or undeserving because they look outside and only see the best in others, yet only see the worst in themselves. I am willing to bet that you have been guilty of doing this very thing in your own life too because no one is immune to this self-sabotaging behavior.

As you grow older and live with your flaws longer, you have two choices — to continue hating them and hiding for fear of being "found out" or to accept them as they are and proceed with your life anyway. If you choose the former, you will only be holding yourself back as chances are no one who truly means anything to your life or to your success will care about your flaws. If you choose the latter, you put the power of your future into your own hands and enable yourself to design your life in any way you want, regardless of what your flaws may look like or how they may impact you. People who are willing to embrace their flaws and accept them as they are, become people who are willing to grow through their challenges and overcome any obstacle that may be set in their path.

Growing accepting over your flaws whether they are physical or hidden in the inner world takes time and practice. You need to be willing to put forth an accepting and patient hand that lends you the

Self-Compassion

support you need to move forward and overcomes your fears of what might happen if people "found out" about your flaws. You quite literally need to be willing to be the person who will lift yourself up so that when you reach the other side of acceptance, it is you who accept yourself and not someone else that you have become dependent on for acceptance. As you can probably imagine, this requires a lot of self-awareness, self-compassion, self-acceptance, and a willingness to be gentle with yourself as you figure out the process and find your way to success.

How you find your own self-compassion and self-acceptance will depend on what your present feelings towards yourself are and how willing to be compassionate towards yourself you are. If you are listening this book, I would imagine that you likely have a great desire to be compassionate towards yourself but realize this — desire does not equal willingness. You need to truly be willing to be unconditionally compassionate and accepting of yourself if you are ever going to make a change in your life or else changes will never truly stick with you.

Some practices you can try include getting realistic with yourself and checking your perception to make sure that you are being honest in your inner communications. For example, if you are continually telling yourself that you are ugly because you have a birthmark on your face, stop and truly consider whether this is true or not. You may not like the appearance of the birthmark, but is that because you have been taught not to love it or because you genuinely do not love it? Is your lack of love towards your perceived flaw because you have been bullied into believing that it made you unworthy, or because someone meaningful to you told you that you would be much more attractive without it? Do you genuinely believe that your birthmark or any other flaw you may possess is the real reason that you are not receiving all that you desire in life? Or is it because you are allowing it to hold you back due to a fear of being seen and truly receiving what you want from life? Maybe the problem is not your flaw, but your fear of what it might take for you to get what you desire and so you use your flaw as an excuse to hold you back.

Think about it, you were not born as a perfect human— you were born as a real human. You were born as a complete person with likes and dislikes, strengths and weaknesses, and various differences that would grow to exist between yourself and the rest of the world. All of us were born this way. Just because you are unique does not necessarily mean that you are quite as different as you may believe you are. It simply means that you are a real human just like the rest of us. Although there may be things that are different about you, there are things that are different about everyone else too. This is something we all share in common. So you see, even though it sounds unlikely, your differences actually make you pretty normal and you deserve to allow yourself to behave in whatever way feels normal to you without having to dance around your perceived flaws along the way. You can safely embrace the fullness of who you are and trust that no matter how bad they may seem, your flaws are never bad enough to result in you being unworthy of anything that life has to offer you.

Accepting Your Future Self

Believe it or not, there is a deep need for you to accept your future self just as much as you need to accept yourself as you are and accept your past as it was. If you don't, you may end up holding your future self to the same unreasonably high standards that you have just let your present and past self off of the hook for. This often happens when you heal your present and past self but fail to analyze your goals and make sure that you are being reasonable towards your future self, too. If you continue holding yourself up to goals that are beyond reasonable or dreams that are unachievable, you are only going to set yourself up for failure when you never achieve them.

Self-Compassion

Now, I'm not saying that your dreams or goals should not be challenging or that anything you truly desire to have is not achievable. After all, airplanes and hovercrafts exist, don't they? Humans really can do anything that they put their mind towards, so technically there is almost nothing that we cannot accomplish as a society or even as individual people. However, people who set big dreams and goals also realize that there is always the chance that their outcome may not look exactly as they had desired for it to look. They may discover instead that all of their efforts ended up leading them down a different path or towards a different future than they had envisioned all along. When this happens, that person can choose to feel like a constant failure because they never achieved the original dream or they can feel grateful to the original dream for giving them the encouragement that they needed to achieve their present success.

See, life will never go the way you plan for it to go, no matter how hard you attempt to stay on track with that plan. You will continually learn new things and discover new information that helps you evolve and grow as a person which means that what you are working towards will evolve and grow too. For example, say you went to school to become a behavioral psychologist and you found that you had a particular attraction towards neuroscience and the brain to the point that you preferred it over your original study of behavioral psychology. Although you may have entered school with the dream of becoming a behavioral psychologist, your introduction to the brain and its functions through those psychology classes resulted in you to realize that you were more passionate about the brain. So, if you were to go ahead and pursue neuroscience and become a brain surgeon, would that make you any less successful? No. It would simply mean that your original plan was changed by the evolution of your life and the unfolding of natural events. If you do not consciously let your future self off of the hook, you may find yourself becoming hung up on the

Self-Compassion

fact that you can never see things through or that you struggle to make up your mind, rather than proud of the fact that you are a brain surgeon.

This is not restricted to large events either which may be easier for you to justify over smaller things that had seemingly less obvious or valuable outcomes than the larger shifts in your life. However, it is imperative that you realize that even the smaller evolutions matter as they are all designed to help you continue moving down a path of life that you genuinely love and that bring you sincere joy and happiness. If you do not let your future self off of the hook for changing your mind and evolving naturally, you may simply find every reason to criticize yourself for changing your mind, even though changing your mind may have been exactly the right thing to do.

A practice regularly used when it comes to accepting your future self in advance is called "releasing the outcome." In other words, you focus on setting the intention for what you desire in your life and you release the outcome by agreeing that if things work out differently than if you had planned, you will still be just as grateful and happy for your success. When you release the outcome, you are not saying that the outcome does not exist or that it is not worthy of pursuing. Instead, you are simply using your present dream and goal as your motivation to move forward and accept that it will change along the way. In this case, your dream or goal becomes a tool to help you continue moving forward and not a finite end result that allows you to determine whether or not you have been successful in your life.

Chapter 4: Silence and Self-Criticism

Most people are fairly unaware of the power that their inner critic has and how drastically it impacts their life. Many believe that the voice of their inner critic or their autobiographical self is finite and true and that everything it says is to be believed and accepted as the ultimate truth. Of course, this is not the case but we are seldom taught to see our inner critic as an untrained inner voice that truly believes it is trying to help us yet has no idea that it is going about it in the wrong way. Think of your inner critic as your overly blunt best friend — they believe they are telling you what you need to hear so that you can do better but in reality, what they say may hurt and result in you feeling unworthy and incapable. In other words, their intentions may be great but their execution is terrible which means that their approach needs to be adjusted. Just like you would with an overly blunt best friend, you need to confront your inner critic and teach it how to start treating you in a more polite and effective manner.

When you learn to master your inner critic and use it to your advantage rather than allowing it to tear you down, your inner critic becomes a powerful tool that you can enjoy in your life. Instead of holding you back or leading to your self-sabotaging behaviors, it starts propelling you forward through life and giving you the support that you need to succeed. Mastering your inner critic can also help you begin enjoying silence in your life more, as you will not spend every moment of silence being filled with the harsh echoes of your inner critic. Instead, your moments of silence will be genuinely peaceful and enjoyable and will support you in feeling even better in your life.

Turning Self-Criticism into a Gentle Supporter

Self-Compassion

Unrelenting self-criticism can be damaging and painful to endure, but not all forms of self-criticism need to be unrelenting and unmanageable. In fact, if you learn how to master your inner critic, it can become one of the gentlest yet effective supports you have in your life. The key is to discover how self-criticism truly can be mastered so that your inner critic is not running rampant and spewing hurtful criticism in your direction at any given moment. Instead, the gentle self-critic is a voice that recognizes opportunities to improve and provides you with self-awareness and understanding that allows you to begin growing in a positive manner, rather than feeling battered by your inner self. As with anything, learning how to embrace your inner self-critic and master it in a way that allows it to become gentle and supportive takes time, patience, and practice.

One way that you can begin to turn your inner self-critic into a gentle supporter is by teaching yourself to criticize behaviors instead of attributes. Unlike attributes, behavior can be changed and improved upon which means that if you are criticizing these, there is actually something that you can do about it to make things better. If you spend all of your time criticizing your attributes, you will always feel like there is nothing that you can do to have a better life because you will always be judging yourself based on things you cannot change. Learning to accept the things that you cannot change and critique and improve on the things that you can is a critical balance that is going to allow you to improve your life in massive ways.

When you are critiquing your behaviors, seek to do so in a way that is productive and effective. Realize that there is a difference between bullying yourself over a mistake and recognizing a mistake and looking for opportunities to improve upon it. If you bully yourself, you are always going to feel as though you are unable to make changes in your life because there is something inherently wrong with you or your previous mistakes mean that you are not deserving of a positive future. This is not constructive in helping you move forward and live a better life. It will only hold you back further. You need to have compassion towards yourself and offer yourself criticism in a way that allows you to actually act upon it and make changes in your life. Seek to empower yourself by pointing out your faults and offering a word of advice, rather than attempting to whip yourself into submission.

A powerful way to confront your inner critic and choose to share in a more compassionate and meaningful way is to look in the mirror and confront your inner critic and all that it has said to you. Recognize that it has always attempted to lead you down the right path and thank it for that, then get clear with yourself about how the criticizing truly feels. Do not be afraid to be honest about how it makes you feel regardless of how painful it may be to admit these feelings to yourself. Speak to your inner critic as if it were another person and be completely clear about how you feel and what you need. When you address yourself in this manner, recognizing your feelings and how damaging your current processes are becomes a lot easier because you bring the emotions and thoughts to light rather than attempting to repress them.

Going forward, each time you hear your inner critic growing harsh and abusive, slow down and remind yourself to approach your need for change in a more compassionate and mindful manner. Take the time to honestly address your feelings and what you believe you need to improve on and then make the conscious effort to begin improving upon those things. Each time you find yourself engaging in your old habit of being mean towards yourself, forgive yourself for that experience and consciously switch the vocabulary so that the criticism comes across more meaningful and polite. For example, say you feel that you struggle to communicate with others and you regularly find yourself wishing that you could share more meaningful and effective conversations with those around you. If your inner critic is unrelenting, it may begin to say things like "I am horrible at communication, I can never say the right things. I can't believe I said that. I must have sounded so stupid. I am so embarrassed about this I should not engage in conversations like this anymore. Clearly, I am incapable." This type of inner dialogue is common but as you can probably see just by reading those words off of the paper, it is mean and hurtful. If you regularly think these things, you will always think that you are incapable and that you must avoid situations where your inabilities shine through such as conversations in this situation. Naturally, conversations are unavoidable so every time you engage in one and these thoughts arise, you will only use it as further evidence that you are unworthy and incapable.

Instead, you could change the dialogue to say something more polite such as "I tried my best, but I definitely think I could have done better. When I said that, I should have been more clear and confident about what I was saying so that I was taken more seriously. I will do better next time so that I can improve on my speaking abilities and have better conversations." Not only is that a significantly more polite way of approaching yourself when it comes to criticism, but it is also done in a way that is actually constructive and supportive. When you give yourself criticism in this way, you reflect on what you felt went wrong and search for a solution immediately so that you can improve in the future. That way, you do not feel as though you are at the mercy of your inabilities because you are clearly focusing on doing better.

Activating Your Growth Mindset

Having a growth mindset means that your focus is always on looking for ways that you can improve yourself and your life. Rather than consistently staying focused on your flaws and setbacks, you focus on the things that you truly can control and then you put in every effort to improve those things. Some people naturally foster a growth mindset over the course of their lives whereas other people have to consciously focus on developing a growth mindset later in life. If you are looking to activate your growth mindset so that you can have more compassion for yourself and focus more deeply on where you can improve your life rather than obsessing over your flaws, the following strategies will help you.

View Your Challenges as Opportunities

A major component of the growth mindset is switching how you view challenges in your life. When you choose to see your challenges as a way for you to improve or move forward in your life, you literally open your mind up to a whole new world of opportunities. Rather than using excuses, victimizing yourself, or complaining every time you see a challenge arise in your life, choose to see it as an opportunity instead. Viewing your challenges as opportunities means that you take away their power to hold you back and prevent you from growing.

Each time you face a new challenge in your life, refrain from asking yourself "why is this happening to me?" and start asking yourself "what is this teaching me?" When you make this simple change in your perspective, seeing the opportunities that each obstacle presents becomes easier and you realize that you have far more options than simple defeat.

Try Learning in New Ways

There are actually four different ways of learning new information — visual, auditory, verbal, and physical. Some people need to see things in clear detail in order to understand them, whereas other people need to physically practice what they are being taught in order to make sense of the information. Everyone can learn in each of these ways but people tend to be more effective at learning in one style over the others.

By discovering what learning style serves you best, you can ensure that you always tailor your learning to that style as much as you can. That way, you are far more likely to absorb what you are learning and genuinely improve your skills rather than feel defeated or like you are incapable of learning the information at hand.

Say "Learning" Instead of "Failing"

Just like you want to reframe your challenges as being opportunities, you also want to reframe your failures as lessons. When you say that something is a failure, you view it as being finite and finished, thus leading you to behave like there is no alternative to the outcome that you have received. People who believe in failure find themselves feeling as though they are always being trampled on by life and like they have no solutions to move forward and create the life that they deserve. They frequently take advantage of excuses as a way to avoid having to try again and often these people genuinely believe that their excuses provide a genuine reason as to why they cannot proceed.

If you want to find yourself regularly being held down by your setbacks and seeing every lesson as a failure, you are going to find yourself offering every excuse under the sun for why you cannot try again. In the end, you will only be robbing yourself of growth potential and preventing yourself from achieving the success that you desire. You need to reframe your failure so that you can begin seeing it as an opportunity to continue learning, rather than a finite ending to something that you deeply desire. You are not unable to move beyond failure and learn from it, you simply need to reframe how you perceive failure so that you can grow past it every single time.

Value the Process More

When you value the outcome, you end up slacking or cutting corners during the process so that you can achieve the success that you desire. What ends up happening is that your success is unsustainable because it is based on things that you do not truly know or understand. Thus, when something inevitably shakes it and you are put in a position where you need to perform, you are unable to perform effectively and everything falls apart. No one wins when you slack on the learning process and jump straight to the outcome.

Furthermore, as you already know, the outcome rarely looks the way you believe it will. If you favor the outcome more than the process, you will completely lose the joy and value in the process because you will be so fixated on what results you were planning on getting out of it. Take your time and invest in the day to day learning, it will serve you a lot more when it comes to finding value in your life and gaining genuine skills that will sustain you for the long haul.

Celebrate Your Growth with Others

Attempting to celebrate your growth on your own can become extremely lonely and fast. When it feels like you are the only one who cares about your growth and success, sometimes it can feel mildly pointless and like it may not be worth it for you to continue pursuing. That doesn't mean that you should make your growth all about receiving positive attention from other people, but inviting other people to celebrate in your growth can make it feel more meaningful and real.

When you take big steps towards celebrating new growth in your life, do not be afraid to invite those who care about you to celebrate your growth with you. Instead of holing up in your house watching a good movie by yourself, invite a good friend or even several good friends out to dinner with you. Celebrate your growth by spending time with the people that you care about and making it truly meaningful as this feels far more rewarding and special than celebrating it alone every single time.

Reward Your Actions Not Your Traits

A major drawback of living in the age of social media is that we have a tendency to see other people's traits and not necessarily their actions or behaviors. What can end up happening is that you find yourself only acknowledging your own traits and comparing them against others as well. Remember, traits or attributes are not things that you can change about yourself — they simply exist as they are.

If you want to really activate your growth mindset, focus on your behaviors and actions and reward yourself for positive behaviors. This will make it easier for you to start focusing on the parts of yourself that you can change and that when changed, can have a tremendously positive impact on your personal growth.

Care about Effort over Talent

Putting too much emphasis on your talents or the talents of others can leave you feeling incredibly judgmental over trivial things. Talent can be cultivated, meaning that anyone can become talented at anything as long as they put their mind to it and truly keep trying. This means that it is not the current level of talent that truly matters, but instead, it is the current level of effort that truly matters. People who are bound for success are going to be focusing on their efforts and putting a large amount of energy into achieving positive results from their efforts. As a result, they are more likely to succeed.

This is also a great tool to use if you are recovering from perfectionism and are working towards releasing yourself from having to get everything right from the start. When you begin to care about your own efforts more than your current level of talent, you begin to open up the energy that you need in order to achieve your desired success without putting so much pressure on yourself for not being the best right away. People who do end up achieving statuses like "the best" do not get there from trying to be perfect right away. They get there from constant, intentional effort.

Take Responsibility for Yourself

You are the only person who is responsible for everything that you have done in your life, not anyone else. Although other people may have contributed to your decisions, at the end of the day, they were not the ones who made those decisions for you, you made them. You need to realize that you are the only one who can take responsibility for yourself. When you do, making the decision to behave in a way that allows you to step out of victim mentality and into the mindset that is required for continuous growth becomes significantly easier.

Starting today, work towards taking responsibility for every single action and decision that you make. Do not let anyone else pressure you into choosing decisions that you did not truly want to make or taking actions that you truly did not want to take. When you take responsibility, you will find that it is much easier for you to then choose to take the actions that *you* want to take such as growing and improving upon yourself.

Self-Compassion

Dealing With Your Mistakes

Everyone makes mistakes. That is just a fact of life. You may have heard the saying before that goes "It doesn't matter what mistakes you make in life, what does matter is how you proceed after making those mistakes." If you make a mistake and you continually make the same mistake repeatedly, then you can guarantee that you are not actively or effectively learning the lessons that you need to in order to generate success in your life. Instead, you are staying trapped in habits and cycles that are preventing you from growing because you refuse to recognize your mistakes and make new decisions. Once again, this is another example of where taking responsibility for yourself and your life becomes valuable. When you take responsibility, you commit to taking the actions required to make a change.

Anytime you make a mistake in your life and find yourself facing results that you do not desire, commit to learning how you can move beyond those mistakes and start generating more positive results from your efforts. As you do, you will begin to find ways that you can learn and grow from your mistakes so that you do not find yourself consistently making the same ones over and over again. You can commit to finding the solution by getting yourself focused on discovering where your efforts went wrong and how you might have handled the situation differently. This allows you to dissect the mistake and see what went right and what didn't, which ensures that you are actually correcting the proper problematic behavior.

After you have discovered where the problematic behavior or action lies, you can start looking for honest solutions that allow you to improve going forward so that you do not repeatedly make the same mistakes time and again. When you give this amount of attention to improving yourself, what ends up happening is that not only do you achieve personal growth but you also achieve personal pride. Rather than feeling embarrassed, frustrated, or defeated by being trapped inside of a habit loop or a behavioral pattern, you can feel confident in your consistent improvements. This gives yourself a sense of hope that you are going to continue doing and achieving better things in life, while also allowing you to remain compassionate towards yourself when your efforts do not pay off immediately. Because you can trust in your own problem-solving abilities and your deep inner desire to change, you can trust that you are not always going to be stuck experiencing the same unwanted situations over and over again.

Aside from looking for your opportunity to improve upon your previous mistakes and making a plan to do so, you should also spend some time forgiving yourself when you have made a mistake in your life. Failure to genuinely forgive yourself can leave you feeling unresolved emotions that can result in you generating deep seeded resentment or mistrust towards yourself. Take the time to address your emotions and feel your way through the situation while also logically planning your next steps so that you can fully complete the cycle of the mistake and start stepping away from it more productively going forward.

Moving on after You've Made an Error

After you have made an error in your life, knowing how to completely move on is imperative. As you know, forgiving yourself and making a plan are two important components of moving forward because this allows you to complete the cycle and feel confident that your solution is effective enough to help you do better next time. There are other things that you should do when you are moving on from an error to help you feel a more complete sense of moving on as well, however.

One thing that you should do is communicate with anyone else who may have been affected by your error to ensure that your intentions

Self-Compassion

and feelings are made clear. This also gives you the opportunity to apologize if an apology is needed which ensures that nothing is left unfinished. If you do not take the time to communicate with others and bring closure to a situation that involves other people, it can generate feelings of resentment, mistrust, and guilt. You may find that the other person struggles to trust you because you were unable to admit to your mistake and that you feel a tremendous amount of guilt around making the said mistake that leaves you embarrassed or afraid of approaching them. This can destroy relationships so bringing in an element of communication and healing any relationships that may have been damaged in the process is important. Doing so will ensure that being compassionate towards yourself is easier because you know that you did everything you could to make the situation better and you were not left feeling guilty or blaming yourself for not apologizing or correcting the situation sooner.

The next thing that you need to do is bring in an element of gratitude so that you can begin seeing the positive in your mistake. For some mistakes, seeing the positive element is going to be challenging because the mistake may have been so large and impactful that you genuinely feel as though nothing good could have possibly come from it. In these situations, look for the things that you have learned following the mistake and see how that mistake has changed your life since happening. These are all things that you can be grateful for even if the mistake itself feels like something so bad that nothing good could possibly come from it.

Anytime you make a mistake in your life, always look to see how it has changed you and how you have grown since the mistake was made. This will help you really begin adopting the growth mindset mentality of nothing being a failure because everything you endure is a lesson. When you are able to embody that mentality and begin exercising it in your real life, allowing yourself to truly grow becomes significantly easier.

Self-Compassion

Letting Go of Overthinking

The final step to overcoming self-criticism and allowing yourself to move on from mistakes that you have made in your life is to make sure that you let go of over thinking. Overthinking can result in you repeatedly going over the same experience in your head over and over again, analyzing every single aspect of the experience, and trying to find new ways to guard yourself against it. Typically, this behavior is intended to help you completely overcome behaviors that have caused you pain or brought you a discomfort in your life, but in the end, it only makes you feel worse. When you over think things, you tend to put far too much pressure on yourself to completely change your behavior in one go to avoid experiencing the same pain that your original mistake brought you. Unfortunately, no one can change all of their behaviors that quickly which will result in you only feeling worse the next time you make a similar mistake because you will feel as though you already had the perfect solution so it is your fault for performing poorly. In reality, you simply had far too high of expectations on yourself so it was virtually impossible for you to measure up to your unreasonable standards.

Not only does over thinking cause you to set unreasonable standards upon yourself, but it also causes you to spend far more time worrying and feeling bad about yourself than you need to. When you are over thinking, you keep a situation in your head far longer than it deserves to actually be there. If you are an avid overthinker, you may find yourself doing this with many different experiences and subjects which leave you feeling even worse and tremendously overwhelmed. Your brain becomes fixated on all of the ways that you believe you are underperforming in life, which can leave you struggling to find any ways that you are performing positively because you are constantly focused on your negative performance.

Simply giving up on over thinking is not always an option. If you have been over thinking for a long time or if you struggle with something like anxiety, then you may find that giving up on over thinking takes a lot of effort. Fortunately, you now know that your emphasis should be focused on the amount of effort that you have put in and not the number of results that you are getting each time. Staying focused on your efforts will ensure that you are focused on making progress which will help you truly achieve your progress in the long run.

The first step to overcoming overthinking is to start becoming aware of how big of a problem overthinking truly is for you. When you begin to practice self-awareness and become aware over how often you are over thinking and how it is making you feel, it becomes easier for you to be honest with yourself about how often you are over thinking things. Through this honesty, you can get clear and realistic on your expectations for how you can improve and what that improvement will look like over time. This way, you do not accidentally set unrealistic expectations on yourself due to a lack of truly being aware of how much your overthinking is impacting you.

Once you are clear on how much you are over thinking and have generated realistic goals on how you can overcome over thinking, you need to start equipping yourself with the necessary tools to break the habit. One great tool is to start teaching yourself to focus on what could go right rather than staying fixated on what could go wrong. While you do still want to be aware of potential problems you may face, also become aware of what positive outcomes you could experience and how they may impact your life. Becoming realistic about all of the possible outcomes including the positive ones helps you to see that every situation has many positive and negative solutions that can be derived from them. Through this, it becomes easier to stay neutral or hopeful rather than negative and fearful around what undesirable outcomes you may encounter along the way.

Self-Compassion

Another way to begin overcoming over thinking is to break the cycle through distractions. When you distract yourself into being happier, your brain learns to start breaking down the cycles that lead to overthinking and literally wires itself into having new habits instead. You can easily distract yourself from over thinking through using positive affirmations, enjoyable hobbies or activities, exercise, or trying something new or different from your usual activities. By breaking out of your normal routine or putting your focus on something more productive, your brain is forced to pay attention which results in you no longer overthinking.

Sometimes overthinking stems from not giving yourself enough time to adequately assess each situation that you are entering. If you are someone who regularly jumps into situations without much thought, or if you used to be like that and you have experienced a tremendous number of unwanted outcomes, you may be afraid to take leaps in your current life. As a result, you may rely on things like overthinking to help you avoid making a significant mistake in the future. What ends up happening, however, is that you find yourself trapped in "analysis paralysis" or in a state where you are unable to stay focused or make a move because you are so afraid of failing. In this circumstance, exercising boundaries is imperative as it will support you in having adequate time to assess your situation and make decisions without feeling pressured to act immediately. For over thinking specifically, set a timer for five minutes analyzing everything that you are afraid of and allowing yourself to think through all of the thoughts that are keeping you worried. Then, set it again for ten minutes so that you can write everything down and get it out of your mind, thus preventing you from feeling as though you have to continually think it in order to avoid "forgetting" about your chosen solution. Once you are done journaling, commit to letting go of the situation and move forward using a tool such as distraction to help you fully disengage from your worry and take actionable steps forward.

Lastly, many people will engage in overthinking as a way to make up for what they feel was a poor performance on their behalf. They believe that by over thinking about the situation and identifying every improvement that they could have possibly made then, in some way, they have retroactively improved their performance and made up for their mistakes. In reality, this is not true. No amount of thinking about alternative outcomes will change the way that the situation unfolded. The best thing that you can do is try your best in every single situation and then pick one or two things you might improve on going forward so that you can have a more positive impact. By staying honest with yourself about how much effort you put in and reasonable with yourself about how much you expect to improve going forward, you can break the cycle of chronic over thinking and move forward positively.

Chapter 5: Mindfulness and Self-Awareness

The final step in fostering a stronger sense of self-compassion is developing your mindfulness and self-awareness. When you develop mindfulness and self-awareness, you equip yourself with the two most important tools required when it comes to improving your relationship with yourself and having a deeper sense of compassion and sympathy towards yourself going forward. People who are more mindful and self-aware have an easier time identifying their self-sabotaging behaviors, putting them into perspective, and moving past them in a productive manner.

In this final chapter, you are going to discover how you can begin building your mindfulness and self-awareness practices in a way that will genuinely support you in feeling a deeper and more meaningful sense of self-compassion. You should seek to implement these practices on a daily basis to ensure that you are always putting in the effort to have a more positive relationship with yourself. As with any relationship in your life, the more genuine attention and care you give to your relationship with yourself, the more you are going to get out of it. Since this is such a personal experience which means that you will experience a greater sense of joy, optimism, self-worth, and self-confidence around your ability to grow and become a better version of yourself every day.

As you go about implementing these practices, remember to embrace deep self-acceptance along the way. Your relationship with yourself may not be where you want it to be right now which may leave you feeling a variety of different emotions such as sadness, pain, anger, and grief. Be patient with these feelings and accept them as they arise

Self-Compassion

so that you can work through them and improve your life going forward.

Practicing Presence

Presence allows you to become more grounded in your current moment and enjoy it for what it is. When you practice presence, you are able to let go of all of your regrets from the past and all of your worries for the future so that you can enjoy the present moment to the fullest of your ability. Through becoming more centered and present, you give yourself the gift of feeling less mental worry and a greater capacity to genuinely receive moments that bring you joy, happiness, and contentment.

Developing your presence is going to require you to deny everything you have ever learned about the getup and go of modern living and start focusing on how you can start slowing down and really embracing each moment as it comes. Instead of constantly checking your calendar or clock for indication of it being time to move onto the next activity, slow down and allow your self to fully immerse into the current one for as long as it lasts. You can do this by setting regular breaks for yourself and committing to completely releasing any unwanted thoughts from your psyche during those breaks, such as thoughts that have you focusing on what comes next or what needs to get done. Once you have released those thoughts, bask in the silence of the moment and start to become aware of what is going on around you right now in the present moment. As you read this even, slow down and take a break so that you can become present in your experience. Notice what is around you, listen to the sounds going on in your environment, and pay attention to any feelings you may be having right now. Getting actively engaged at the moment brings you out of your thoughts and into the experience so that you can start freeing up mental space and enjoying your life more fully.

If you find that you are the type of person who constantly doubles, triple, and quadruple check your watch or phone for an indication that it is time for you to move on to the next activity, look for a more productive way to manage your time. Rather than constantly feeling a nagging to check the time, set an alarm or a reminder that will go off a few minutes before you need to switch activities. This way, you can completely let go of the need to check the time over and over again and start focusing on being present. Instead of the constant distraction, you can trust that you are going to be informed of your next activity with plenty of time without you having to personally pay attention to the time itself.

Lastly, developing a meditation practice is a great way for you to practice releasing your busy mindset habits and start focusing on the present moment. When you develop a meditation practice you give yourself the opportunity to intentionally slow down and practice presence through your meditation. Research suggests that just 10 minutes of meditating each day, ideally in the morning, will support you in having a greater ability to feel more at peace while also staying more present from moment to moment.

Feeling Deeply and Moving On Completely

A highly valuable practice you can use to start developing a deeper sense of mindfulness and self-awareness is to start allowing yourself to deeply feel before moving on completely. In many instances, we find ourselves feeling busy, rushed, and disengaged from every situation that we encounter because we are struggling to fully feel every experience that we have in our lives. When you struggle to feel things deeply, your mind attempts to hold on to those memories and emotions so that you can revisit them at a later time. When you never give yourself that later time, you find yourself holding on to too many things inside of you so you struggle to fully sink into each moment and emotion which keeps you in the cycle of never fully feeling and releasing.

In order to help you deepen your presence and have better experiences in life, begin fostering the art of feeling deeply and releasing completely. Each time you engage in a new moment or feel a new emotion arise, allow it to completely wash over you and feel it to the very depths of what it is. This does not necessarily mean that you need to act on every single emotion to the maximum extent that you can. Instead, just focus on acknowledging it and how far it goes and allow it to really sink into your heart and body as a true and genuine emotion that you are experiencing. If you are in a place where it is safe to do so, do not be afraid to let your emotions out completely by crying, yelling, punching a pillow, or simply lying down and feeling the despair wash through you. Once you have completely felt the depths of the emotion, allow it to be released completely. Since you have felt it completely, releasing it completely is easier because there is nothing residing within you that keeps you attached to that emotion.

If you do find that you are somewhere that seems unacceptable for you to release your emotions such as at work or in an important meeting, give yourself permission to file them away for later. When you do, always make sure that you come back to that emotion as soon as it is reasonable for you to do so and feel into it completely so that you can also release it completely. By setting the intention to dig into and feel that emotion all the way, you ensure that it does not fester and result in you experiencing it any more than you need to.

The Value of Daily Reminders

As you go about changing your habits to incorporate for more mindfulness and self-awareness, nothing will prove to be more valuable than the very simple tool of daily reminders. Having daily reminders in your life to support you in remembering to engage in a mindfulness practice or become aware over your present state of being can support you in actually remembering to engage in and reinforce your new positive habits. The more you see your reminders and engage in your mindfulness and self-awareness, the easier it will be for you to start reminding yourself to engage in these behaviors as well. Over time, you will find that your inner ability to remember and then actually fully engage will improve, allowing you to experience more joy and positivity from your life.

There are many ways that you can set daily reminders for yourself so that you actually pay attention and listen to them. The best way is to set daily reminders in a variety of different ways so that you are actually paying attention and following those reminders as seeing the exact same reminder too often may lead to you ignoring it. You can set reminders on your phone to periodically remind you throughout the day, leave post-it notes around your home and office, and even write it down in your calendar.

Another creative way to remind yourself to engage in mindfulness is to set triggers that are meant to help remind you spontaneously. For example, maybe you decide that from now on every single time you see the color orange you are going to pause for a moment and begin practicing mindfulness and self-awareness. By setting triggers like this, you ensure that you are going to practice mindfulness at all times and not just when you see the reminder on your phone go off or the note in your day timer each morning.

The more reminders you set and the more you commit to actually acting on those reminders, the easier it will be for you to get the fullest value out of them. Over time, you will become so used to these reminders that you will naturally begin engaging in mindfulness and self-awareness all on your own. Any time you notice an intense wave of emotion or a challenging situation surface before you, you will slow down and tap into your mindfulness and self-awareness practices so that you can begin feeling more positive overall. This will continue to develop as you continue to improve your growth mindset which will ultimately lead to you experiencing a continually more positive life experience overall.

Meditation for Mindfulness and Self-Reflection

There are many meditations that you can practice for mindfulness and self-reflection, including the two following ones that I have provided for you. The first one is a shorter meditation that you can practice on the go any time you find yourself feeling intense emotions or energies rushing through your body and find yourself needing to check in with yourself. The second is longer and gives you a more intentional and meaningful connection with yourself so that you can really tune into your inner feelings and process them more effectively. You should seek to use each of these daily, as they will both provide you with great value in improving your overall mindfulness and self-awareness and help you to feel a deeper sense of peace and calm in your life.

A Quick Breathing Meditation

In order to practice this quick breathing meditation, you simply need 2-3 minutes of personal time and a willingness to tune in and fully listen during that period of time. Then, all you need to do is sit or stand somewhere that you will not be distracted and straighten out your posture. Focus on elongating your back, dropping your shoulders, letting your tongue muscles relax, relaxing your core, and fully embracing a moment of peace. When you have completely relaxed your body, take a few deep breaths in and out, counting to four with

Self-Compassion

each inhalation and counting to four with each exhalation, aiming to take at least ten complete breaths.

After you have taken your breaths, ask yourself "How am I feeling right now?" and "What do I need right now?" Listen to the answers that arise so that you can get a clear sense of what emotions arise for you and what needs you may have that are not presently being met. Then, completely acknowledge your emotions and your needs and create a plan to feel through your emotions and fulfill your needs as soon as you possibly can. By acknowledging what you are feeling and what you need and creating a plan to address these two things, you assure yourself that there is no need to worry or feel neglected because you are actively seeking to improve your present conditions.

If you are in a moment where you can actively feel through your emotions or meet your needs, do so right away. If you aren't, be very diligent about coming back to your emotions and needs at a later time and fulfilling them completely as this will allow you to begin developing a sense of trust in yourself and your ability to take care of yourself completely.

A Full Body Scan Meditation

The full body scan meditation is one that you should attempt to accomplish on a daily basis. One great body scan every day, ideally at night time, is a great opportunity for you to check in with yourself, get a sense of what is going on within your mind, and tap into any emotions or thoughts that may be unresolved from the previous day. Consider this as your opportunity to show yourself compassion on purpose particularly if you have been having troubles showing compassion for yourself throughout the day. As you begin to give yourself this quality time and pay attention to yourself on a more

Self-Compassion

consistent basis, you will find that you begin cultivating a deeper relationship with yourself that allows you to tune in even more.

To begin your body scan, simply begin by sitting or lying down and taking several deep breaths into your diaphragm. Fill up your lungs as completely as possible, allowing yourself to relax into each breath as you take it for as long as possible. Once you feel yourself entering a state of relaxation, begin drawing your awareness into your body and seeing if you notice any specific areas that are filled with tension. If you do, go through those areas one by one and make a conscious effort to relax them completely before you begin with your official body scan.

With your body completely relaxed, go ahead and draw your consciousness into your feet and take a moment to notice if you are carrying any tension in them before intentionally relaxing them completely. Then, draw your awareness up into your shins and consciously become aware of any tension you may be carrying there and release it completely, too. Continue doing this all the way up your body by drawing your awareness to your knees, thighs, glutes, hips, abdomen and lower back, torso, middle back, chest and upper back, shoulders, biceps, forearms, hands, neck, and head. By consciously drawing awareness into each of your body parts and letting that awareness rise up through you, you give yourself the opportunity to intentionally release any stress that you may be carrying within your body. This is known as a complete body scan or a form of progressive muscle relaxation that allows you to completely de-stress your entire body and release anything that you may be carrying within you. Once you are done, be sure to address any feelings that may have come up along the way and allow yourself to completely process them and then release them so that you are capable of moving forward completely.

Mindfulness Exercises for You to Try

In addition to meditation, there are many other mindfulness practices that you can try to help you enter a deeper state of mindfulness and self-awareness. These practices range from things that you can actively use to make yourself more consciously aware during your day to day experiences or that you can engage in during your personal time to improve your mindfulness.

Spontaneous Environmental Check In

A spontaneous environmental check-in is a simple practice whereby you slow down and pay attention to the environment around you as you engage in any form of day to day experience. You can do this anytime you notice that you are checking out or struggling to stay grounded in the moment or simply to see just how tuned in you really are. This can be done at work, when you are spending time with friends, or even when you first open your eyes in the morning. The more you practice it, the more mindful you will become.

In order to practice your spontaneous environmental check-in, you simply need to tune into your environment and notice at least one thing that is stimulating each of your senses. So, you want to notice one thing that you see, one thing that you hear, one thing that you feel, one thing that you smell, and one thing that you taste. Since you are likely not tasting your environment at all times, taking a sip of water or chewing a stick of gum is a great way to engage your sense of taste during experiences where you are not actively eating or drinking something as a part of your experience.

Self-Compassion

Mindful Listening Practices

Listening is a powerful tool that can help you really plug into your environment. A great listening practice that can be done in your personal time is called mindful listening and it requires you to use a piece of music or composure to help you engage in mindful listening. The goal as you listen to this music is to listen to each word and actively let each word go as you move onto the next word in the song. Rather than attempting to remember what has been said or formulate an opinion or understanding around what the song means, simply listen to it and experience it in complete presence.

Focusing On Your Details

If you are struggling to stay present or mindful during any particular experience, practice focusing intently on your details. In order to do so, simply bring your awareness into the details of what you are doing. For example, if you are washing dishes, pay attention to the temperature of the water, the texture of the soap, and the visual of watching the dish become clean. Allow yourself to pay close attention to each step of the process and really immerse yourself into how it feels for you so that you can get deeply engaged in the process. By really embracing each detail of the process, you encourage your mind to stay focused on what you are doing rather than allowing it to grow bored and get distracted by other things that may be going on around you.

Self-Reflection Exercises for You to Try

Self-reflection is a great opportunity for you to improve your self-awareness and develop a deeper understanding around who you are and what you have to offer. Practicing self-reflection on a daily basis gives you the opportunity to both understand yourself on a deeper level and decide what you may wish to improve upon in your life so that you can experience greater results from your self-improvement efforts. You should seek to engage in at least one self-reflection exercise per day so that you can really immerse yourself into your growth and learning, as well as cultivate a strong relationship with yourself.

Self-Reflection Journaling

Nothing beats a good old fashioned journal when it comes to learning how to improve upon yourself and become the best version of yourself that you possibly can. Self-reflection journaling is an easy activity that you can engage in on a daily basis so that you can pay attention to how you are doing and really dig into areas of your life that you want to improve on.

The best way to utilize your self-reflection journal is to write down all of the things that you wish you had done better in your day and all of the things that you are exceptionally proud of. For the things that you wish you had done better, write about why you wish you had done better and how you wish you had done things differently. That way, you have an idea of what you can do in the future as well as a clear understanding as to why it happened so that you can practice true compassion with yourself. For the things that you are proud of, celebrate yourself and take a moment to deeply immerse into your pride around these subjects.

Listening In On Your Self-Talk

Eavesdropping on your self-talk is a great way to listen to how you are communicating with yourself and get a better idea on how you can improve the way that you are speaking to yourself. When you listen in on your self-talk, you can get clear on how it may be helping or hindering your success in life. If your self-talk is compassionate and caring, then chances are you are engaging in positive self-talk that is actually supporting you in moving forward in life. However, if your self-talk sounds harsh or condescending, you can easily regain control over it and move back into a state of deeper compassion so that you are no longer attempting to bully yourself into submission.

Tracking Your Progress

The best way to track your progress when it comes to personal development, especially around things like mindfulness and self-awareness which tends to be challenging to measure is through snapshot journaling. Snapshot journaling essentially requires you to write one journal entry per week where you get very honest about how you are currently embracing mindfulness and self-awareness in your life. Be very clear about how well you think you are doing and make sure to highlight any areas where you feel that you are not performing as well as you believe you could be.

By honestly capturing how you are feeling in regards to mindfulness and self-awareness or any other aspects of yourself that you are trying to improve on, you give yourself clear progress notes to look back on. You can then read back through your snapshots and see just how much you have changed and how far you have come based on the notes you have taken. Of course, based on the nature of how this works, you will only get incredible results if you stay highly honest with yourself and truly capture the reality of how you are doing each time.

Another way that you can track your progress is to communicate with a loved one who knows you well. By asking for feedback and requesting them to reflect on your growth as far as they have seen, you also give yourself the opportunity to get a clear understanding of your persona and how it may be reflecting your personal improvements. Be sure not to ask too often or it may become overwhelming or ineffective, but do not be afraid to ask from time to time just to get a clear understanding of how far you have come and where you may need to improve on going forward.

Conclusion

Congratulations on seeing your own personal journey of *Self-Compassion* all the way through until now! While I know your personal journey with cultivating self-compassion will never truly come to an end, our journey together for this book is. Before you go, however, I want to make sure that you truly feel equipped with all of the tools that you need to completely embrace your new skill of self-compassion.

First, I want you to recall the importance of your relationship with yourself and the reality of how your identity is created between three states of awareness that we all possess. I hope that in learning this concept that you were able to develop a stronger understanding of how your perception of who you are and who you truly are will never fully line up. Likewise, how other people see you and who you truly are will never fully line up, either. You are a human with many qualities, characteristics, and aspects to your identity, each of which extends far beyond any one person's perception.

By realizing that your identity is far larger than what you or anyone else thinks of you, I hope you understand how to develop a deeper sense of self-compassion by recognizing that you are not able to be chalked up to any one label. You are by no means incapable, worthless, mean, pathetic, useless, or any other labels that you may be cruelly identifying yourself against. Likewise, you are not any one positive label. In fact, you are many things and in many different ways and who you are change depending on who you are around and what persona you are embracing at that moment. Although there are many constants in who you are, there are also many evolving pieces of your identity that contribute to the reason as to why "who" you are is such a challenging thing to summarize.

Self-Compassion

When you stop trying to identify yourself as any one thing and you open your mind up to the concept that you are many things and nothing all at the same time, it becomes easier for you to stop attaching yourself to labels. In that, you give yourself the freedom you require to begin developing a deeper and gentler connection with yourself and all aspects of your inner identity. The more you detach from labels and the belief that you are one finite identity, the more you will find yourself feeling the freedom to love yourself deeply and intensely.

The second thing I want you to take away from this book is that your self-compassion is something that will evolve over time so do not worry if you have reached this point and you do not yet feel a deep sense of compassion for yourself. The more you practice the tools that I have provided you with here in this book, the more you are going to feel a deeper sense of compassion towards yourself. At first, that sense of compassion may barely crack through the surface of everything that you are feeling and the shell that you keep yourself protected by. However, the more you practice, the deeper your compassion towards yourself will become and the easier it will be for you to hold space for yourself and accept yourself as you really are.

Always be willing to accept yourself for where you are at in your journey and have faith that you will improve as you move forward. Remember, it is okay not to be okay and it is okay to feel like you are not where you wish you were in life. If you feel frustrated, sad, or defeated because you are not further ahead in life, that is okay. Accept yourself as you are and for the emotions you have around what you are going through each day and through that acceptance, it will feel easier for you to heal and move forward.

www.ingramcontent.com/pod-product-compliance
Lightning Source LLC
Chambersburg PA
CBHW030329100526
44592CB00010B/619